MW01625510

For Kevin
who remembers
and Tala
who was not yet born
when all this happened

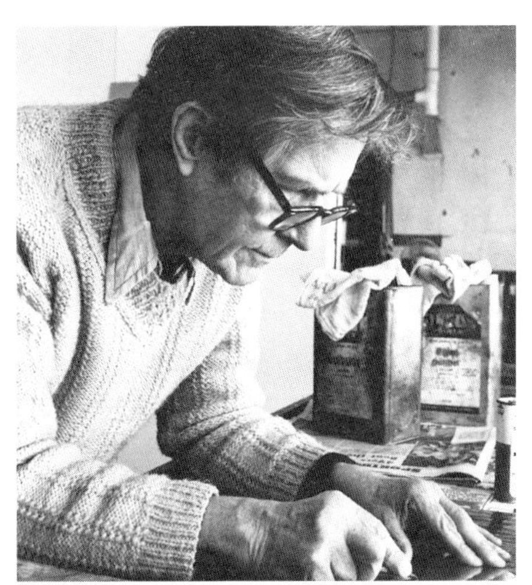

Method

Structure

Intention

Discipline

Notation

Indeterminancy

Interpenetration

Imitation

Devotion

Circumstances

JOHN CAGE

VISUAL ART:

To SOBER and QUIET the MIND

KATHAN BROWN

CROWN POINT PRESS

ISBN 1-891300-16-4
An abridgment of the text will appear in 2002 as a chapter in
The Cambridge Companion to John Cage,
Cambridge University Press, United Kingdom.

Book design by Kathan Brown with Tom Marioni and Sasha Baguskas.
Production by Sasha Baguskas at Crown Point Press.
Photographs of John Cage by Colin McRae, 1982.
The Mesostics by John Cage on pages 11 and 141
are from "Composition in Retrospect" published in
John Cage Etchings 1978-1982 by Crown Point Press, 1982.
The prose quotations from John Cage on pages 12 and 142 are both
on page 129 of *Musicage: John Cage in Conversation with Joan Retallack,*
Wesleyan University Press, 1996.

Printed in the United States of America.

Crown Point Press
20 Hawthorne Street
San Francisco, CA 94105
www.crownpoint.com

ABOUT THIS BOOK

Years ago, before we had a remote control for our television at home, my husband, Tom Marioni, used a long bamboo pole to reach the controls from his chair. John Cage, who stayed with us when he was working on his prints, called the pole Tom's "hunting and fishing stick." I'm hoping this book will be a hunting and fishing stick for you to find your way around in Cage's art. The book has three layers: pictures, ordinary text, and—in a separate section—detailed text. Whichever parts you use, I hope you will get a glimpse of the pleasure Cage took in everything. He hoped that his work would help people to enjoy life, to see and hear more acutely, and to quiet the mind's chatter. "I'm not interested in critical or negative action," he said. "I'm interested in doing something that seems to be useful." Following his example as well as I can, I offer this book as something I hope will be useful to you.

I have had a great deal of help. Margarete Roeder, Cage's art dealer and friend, has provided advice, information, and the photographs we used of *HV2* and of the Plexigram, the drawings, and the watercolors. The Achenbach Foundation for Graphic Arts has provided the thirty-eight photographs of *Déreau*. Joan Retallack, whose interviews with Cage I often quote, read an early draft and helped me shape it; the final draft of the text benefited from further shaping by Editor Judith Dunham. Some of the material in this book will appear in *The Cambridge Companion to John Cage* in 2002, and David Nicholls, who is editing that volume, has made suggestions that improved this one.

The detailed section of text could not have been so detailed without the assistance of Lilah Toland, Andrew Culver, and Leo Holub. The pictures could not have been so beautiful without the care and special attention of Colin McRae, who photographed the prints (and also, long ago, Cage himself) and Rick Levy who did the scanning and color correcting of the photographs. Thanks are due, also, to Carl Solway for information about the Plexigrams, and June Felter and Adrienne Fish for loaning us art to photograph.

Every member of our staff at Crown Point has been engaged in one way or another with this book's production. Thanks are due to all, but especially to Mari Andrews, who helped me make sense of Cage's maps and scores, and to Valerie Wade, Daria Sywulak, and Dena Schuckit who read the manuscript and gave me suggestions that improved it.

Finally, my most practical and indispensable help has come from Tom Marioni, who advised me at every turn, and Sasha Baguskas, our publications coordinator here at Crown Point—she has given me invaluable advice in regard to both content and design, and she has done most of the work. She has produced the book with dedication and skill.

A NOTE ABOUT SEEING THE ART: There is no substitute for the real thing. Karin Breuer, curator of the Achenbach Foundation for Graphic Arts, a part of the Fine Arts Museums of San Francisco, has organized a John Cage exhibition at the California Palace of the Legion of Honor in San Francisco, on view from December 20, 2000 through April 15, 2001. The Achenbach Foundation owns the largest collection of Cage artworks in the United States, including the complete set of *Déreau*, and if you missed the exhibition you can visit their print study room by appointment. (They have everything on their website at www.thinker.org.)

The National Gallery in Washington D.C. also has a representative collection of Cage's prints. The complete set of *Changes and Disappearances* is in the Hyogo Prefecture Museum of Modern Art, Kobe, Japan. The compete sets of both *On the Surface* and *HV2* are in the Erzbischöfliches Diözanmuseum in Cologne, Germany, and there are many other museums, including the Philadelphia Museum of Art, the Block Museum at Northwestern University, and the Nassauischer Kunstverein, Wiesbaden, Germany, that own a number of Cage's works of visual art.

—KB

aCt
In
accoRd
with obstaCles
Using
theM
to find or define the proceSs
you're abouT to be involved in
the questions you'll Ask
if you doN't have enough time
to aCcomplish
what you havE in mind
conSider the work finished

"What I'm proposing, to myself and to other people, is what I often call the tourist attitude—that you act as though you've never been there before. So that you're not *supposed* to know anything about it. If you really get down to brass tacks, we have never been *anywhere* before."

DÉREAU
1982

Thirty-eight engravings with drypoint, aquatint and photoetching printed in two impressions each by Lilah Toland at Crown Point Press.
14 x 18" (36 x 46 cm).

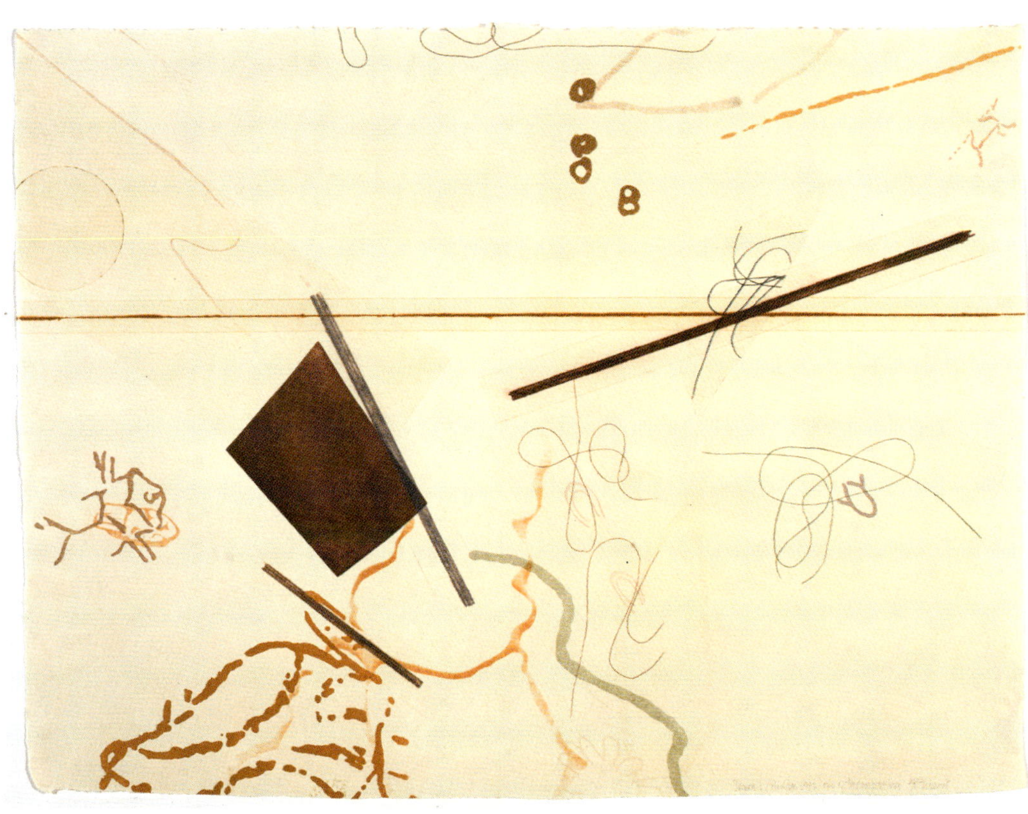

1

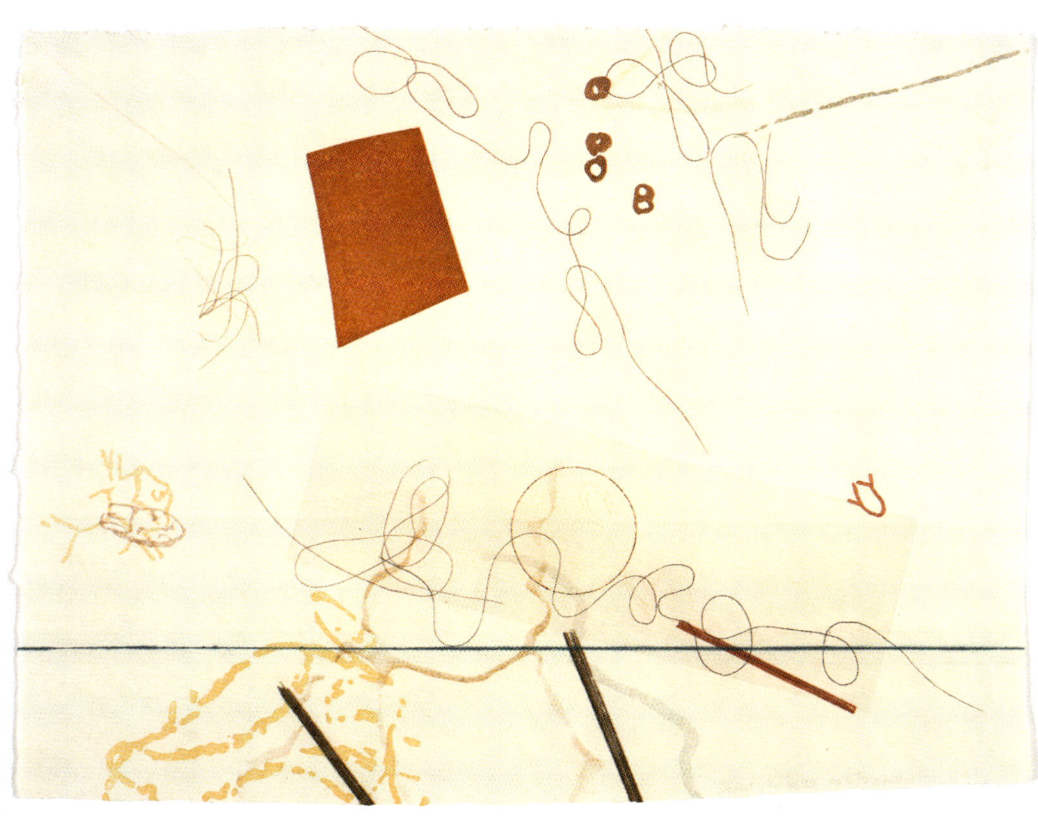

2

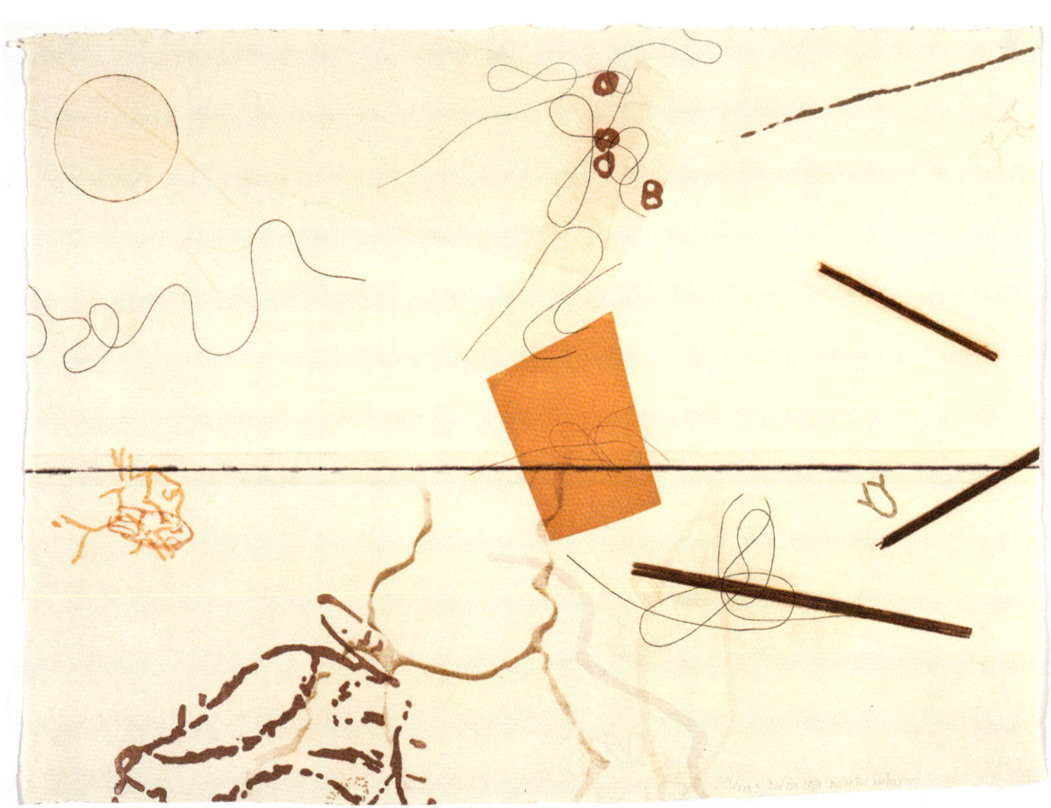

3

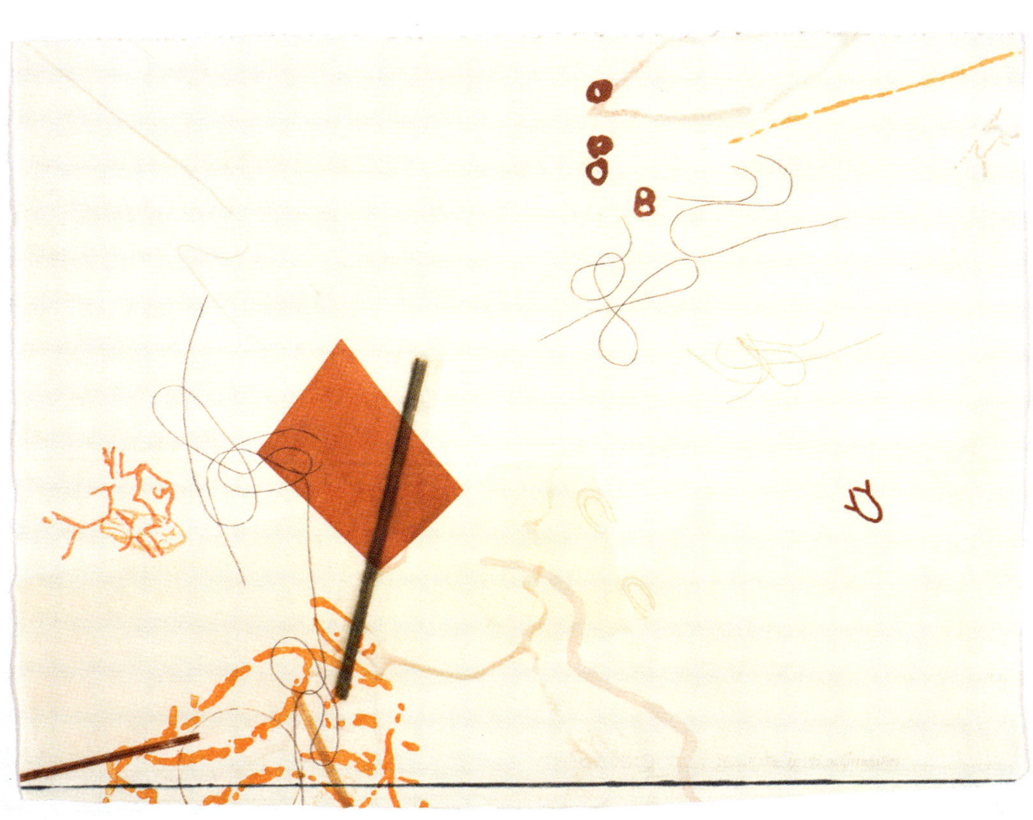

4

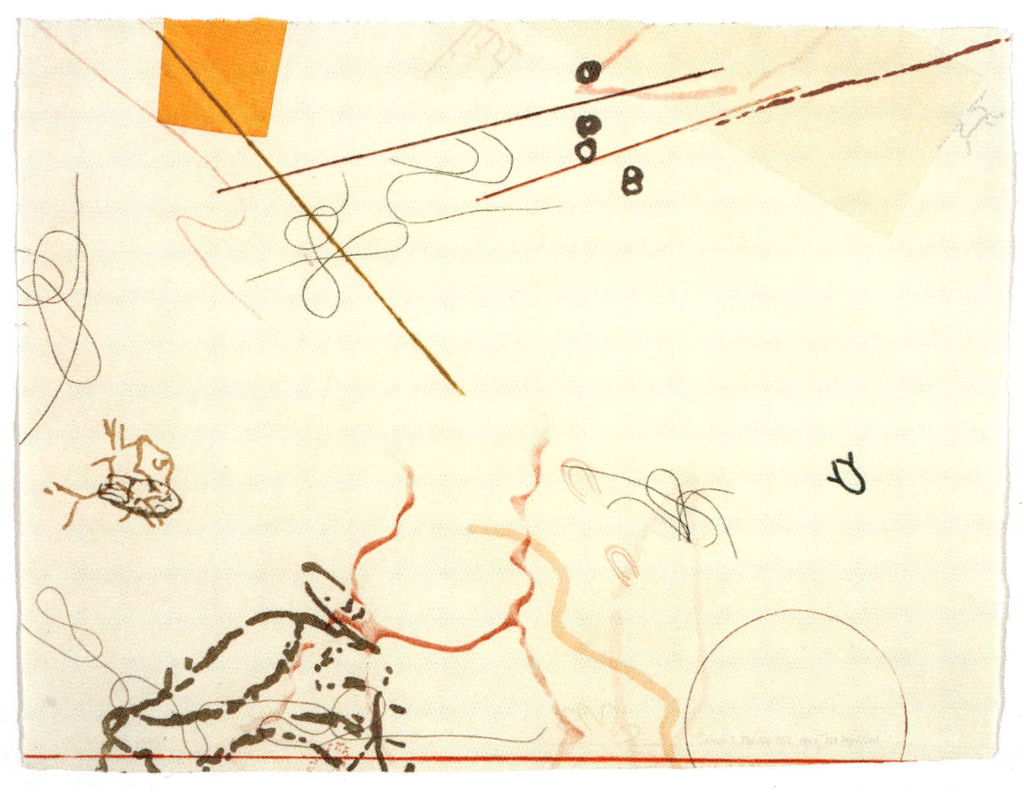

5

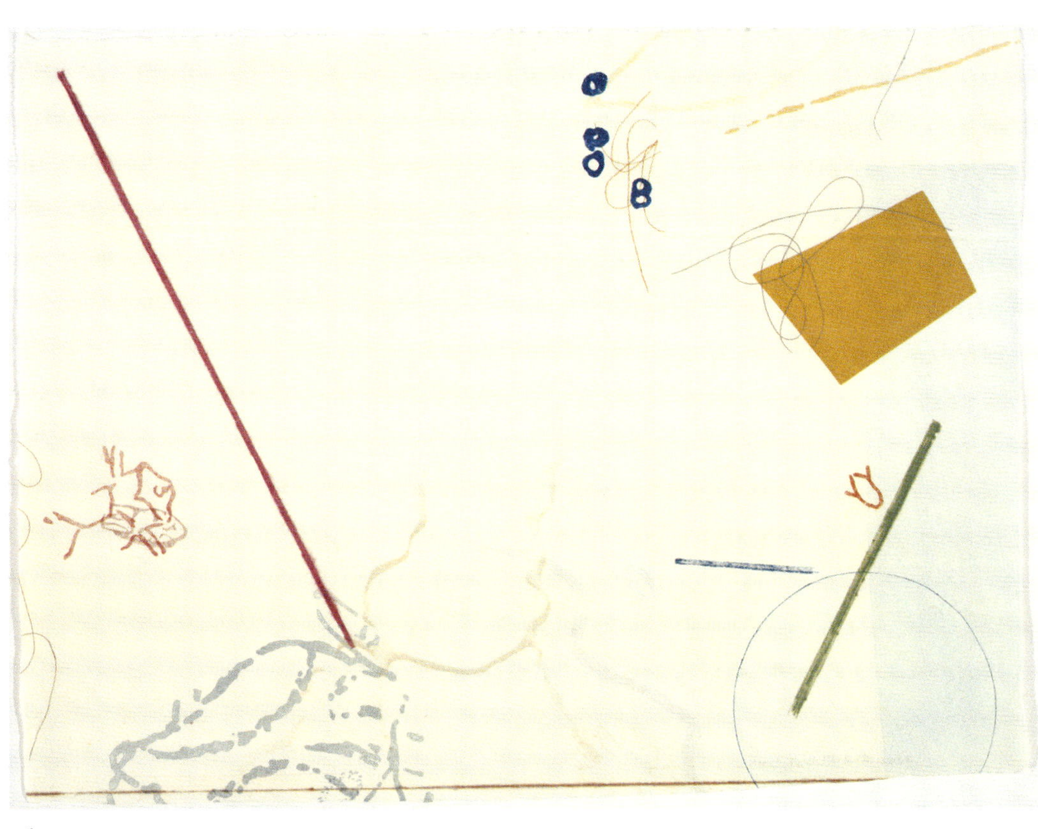

6

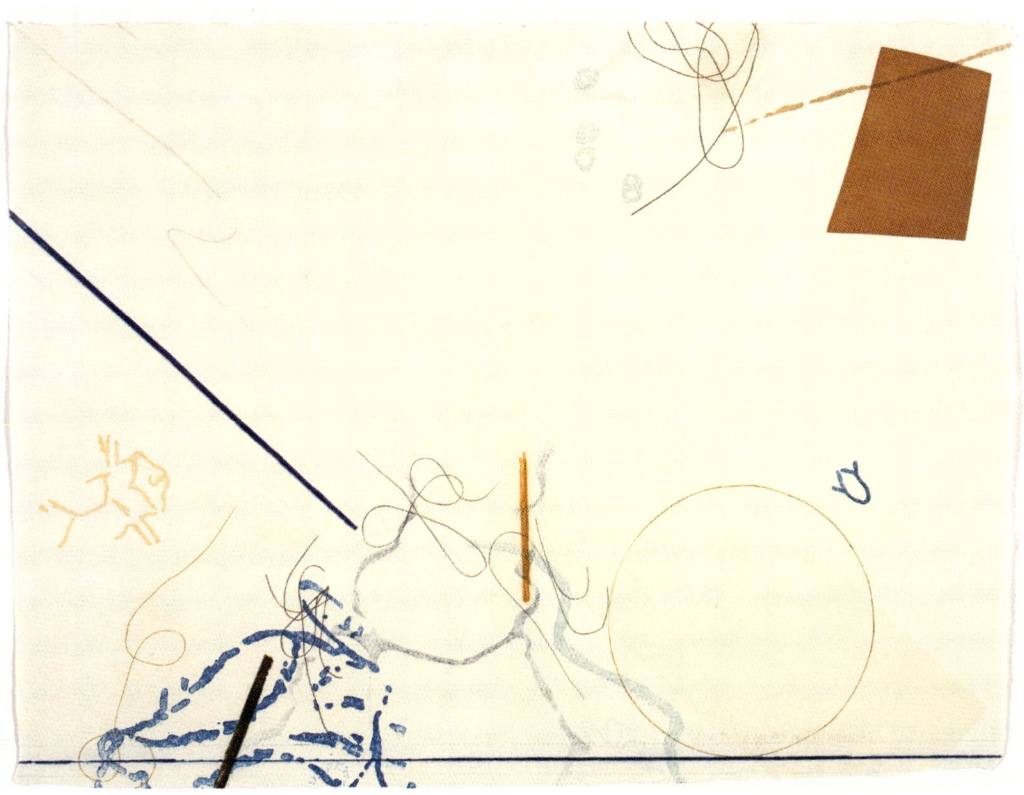

7

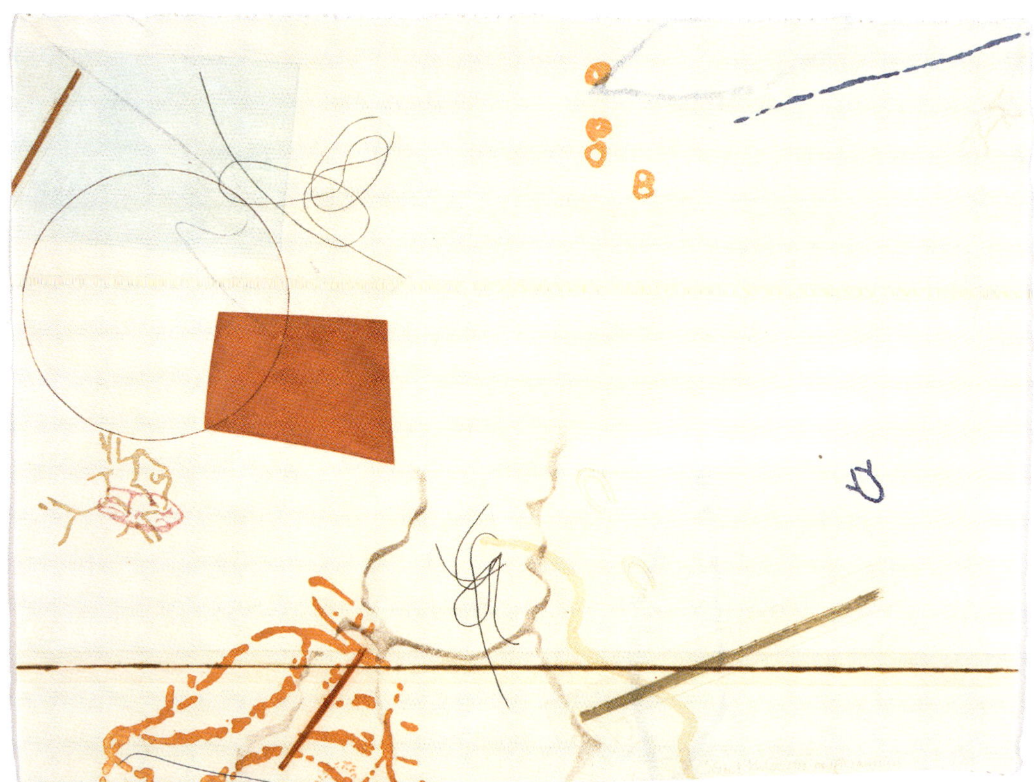

8

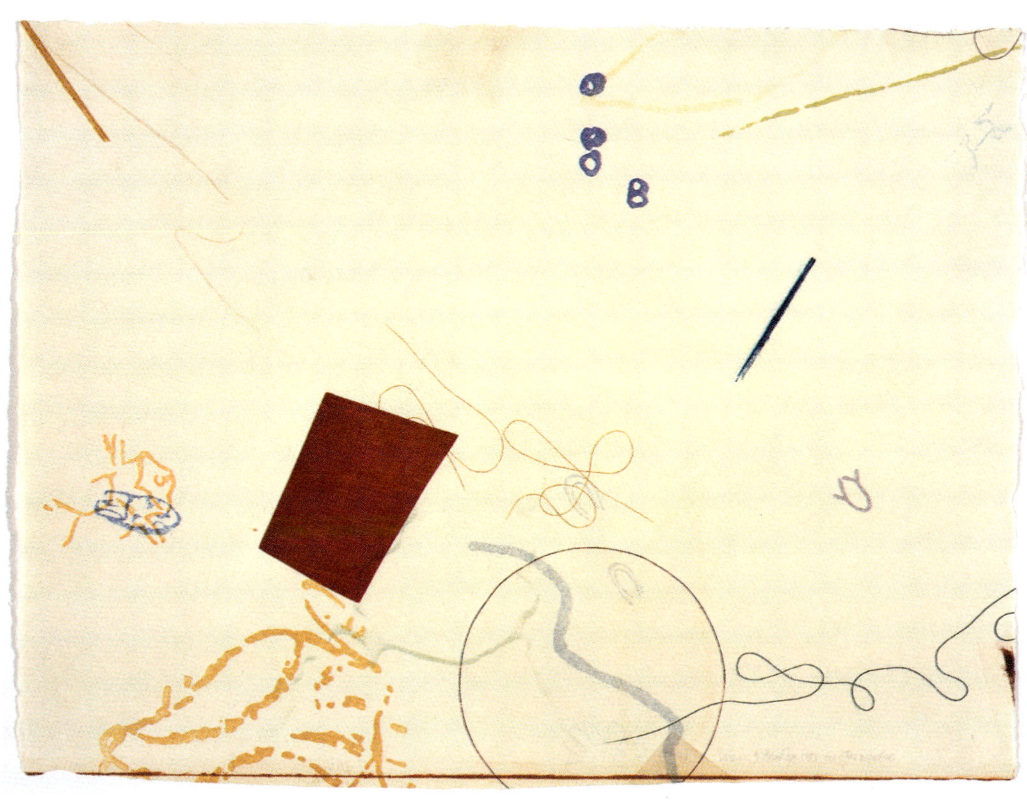

9

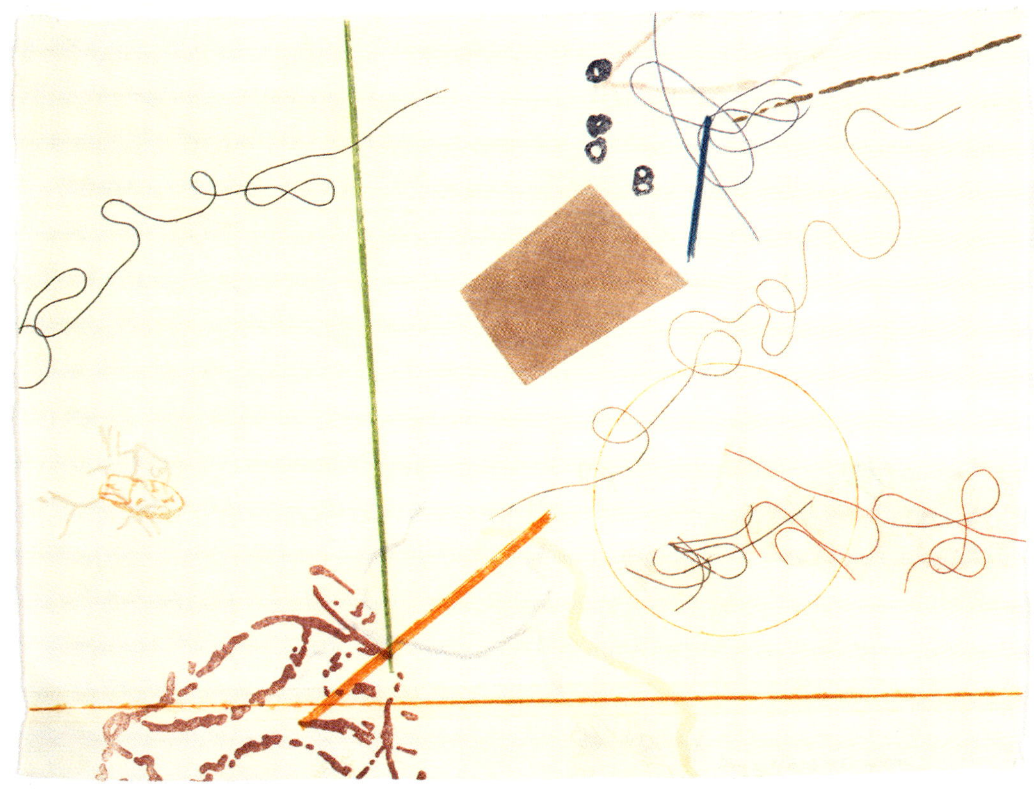

10

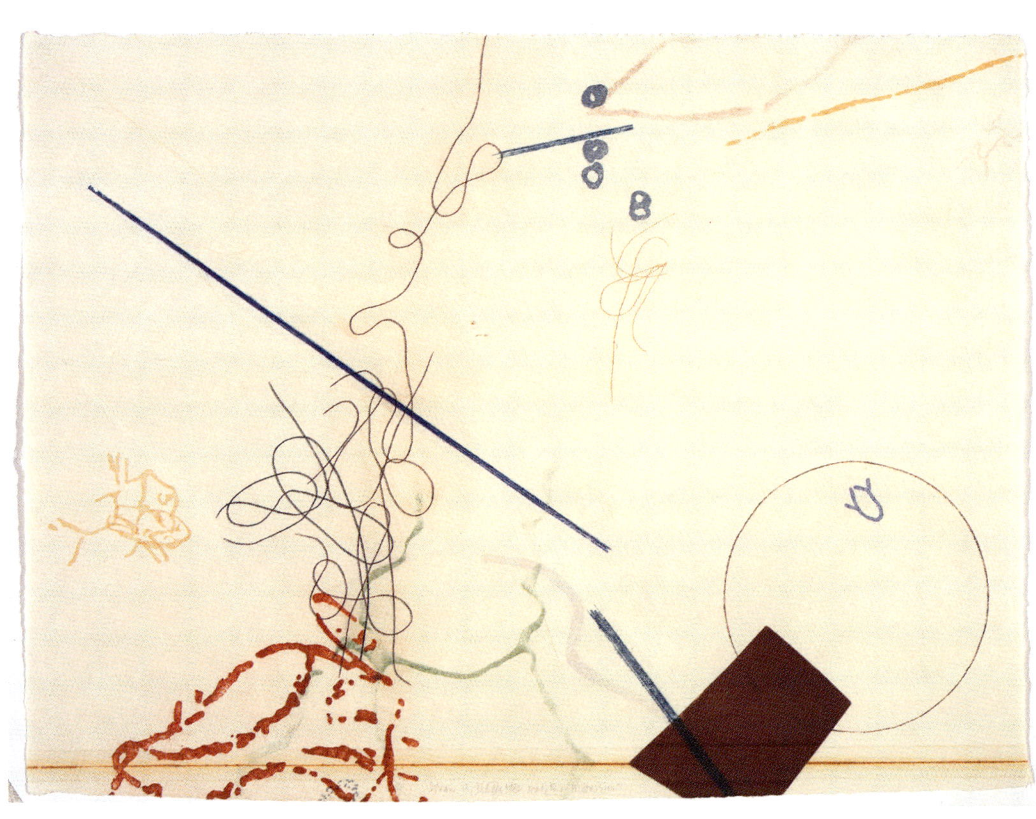

11

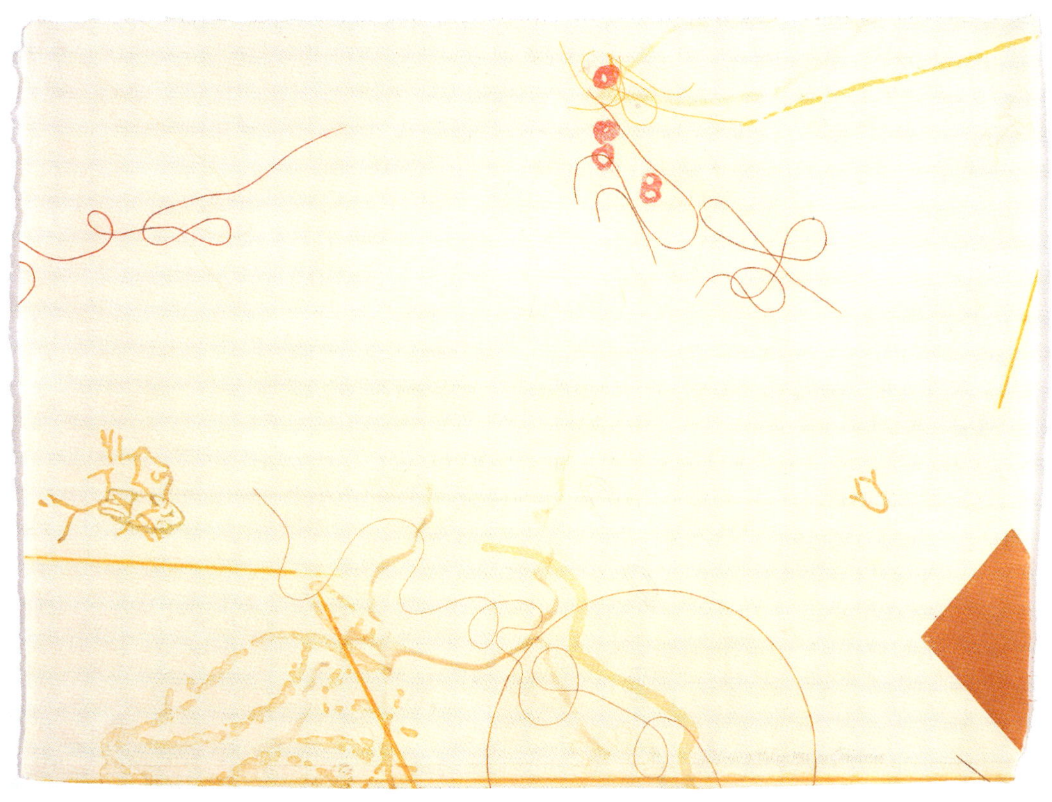

12

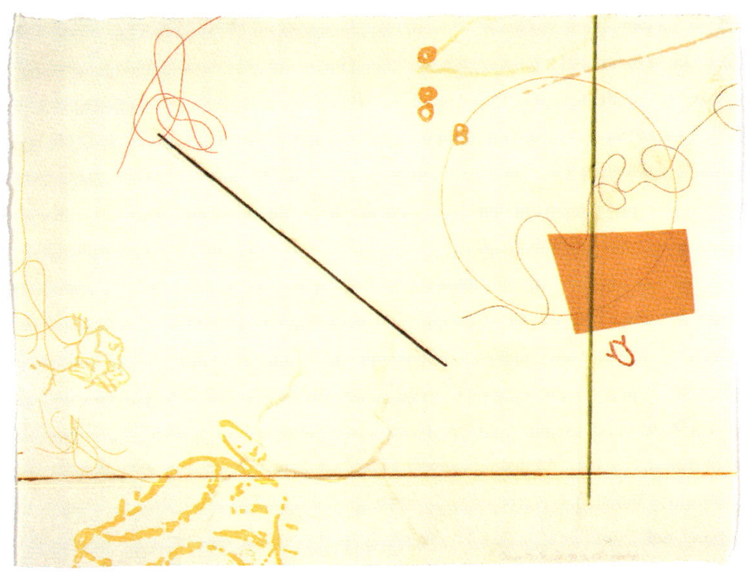

13

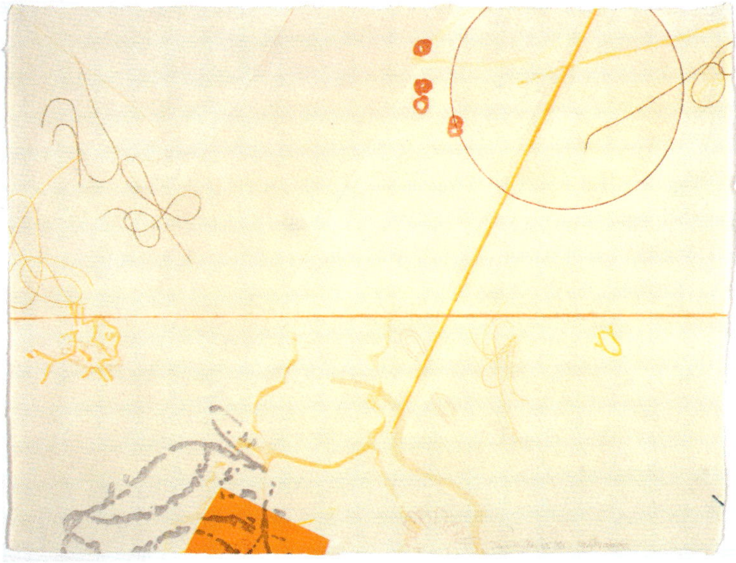

14

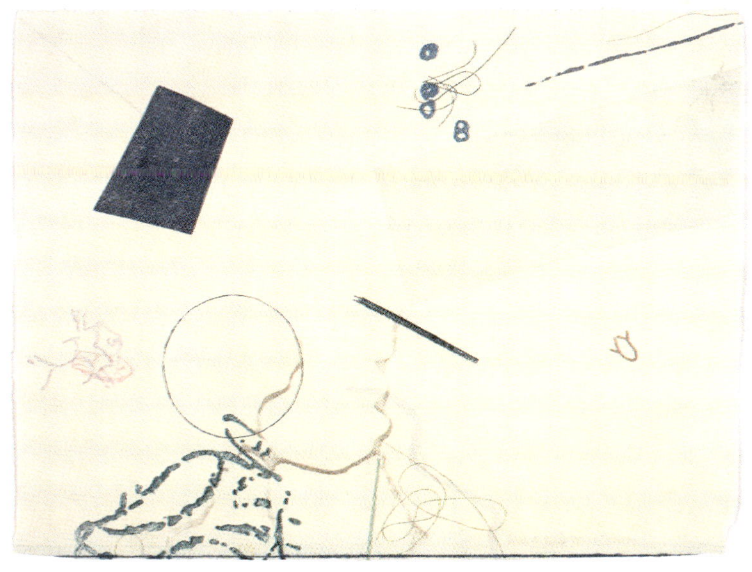

15

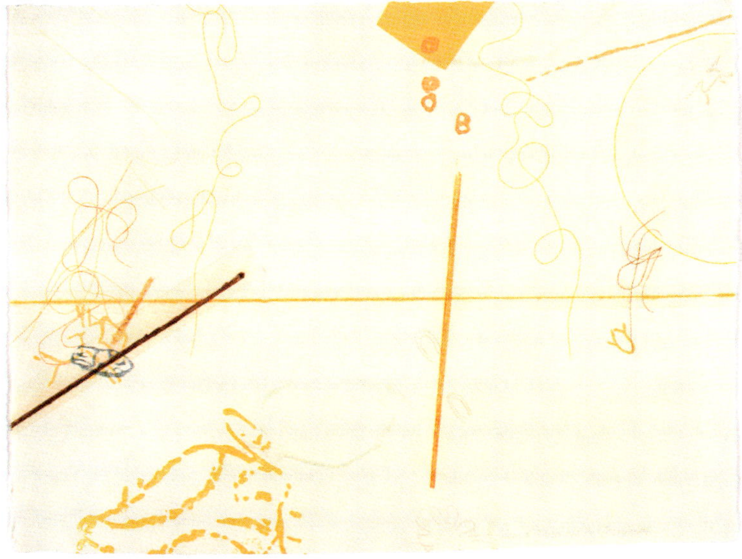

16

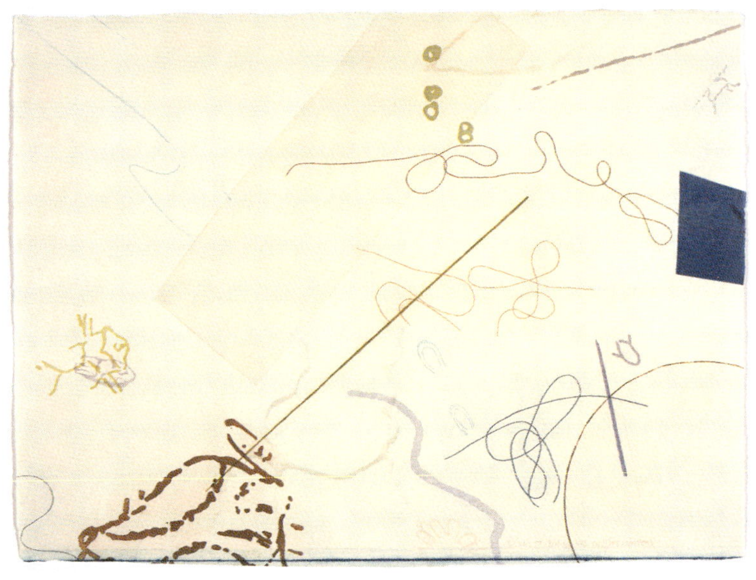

17

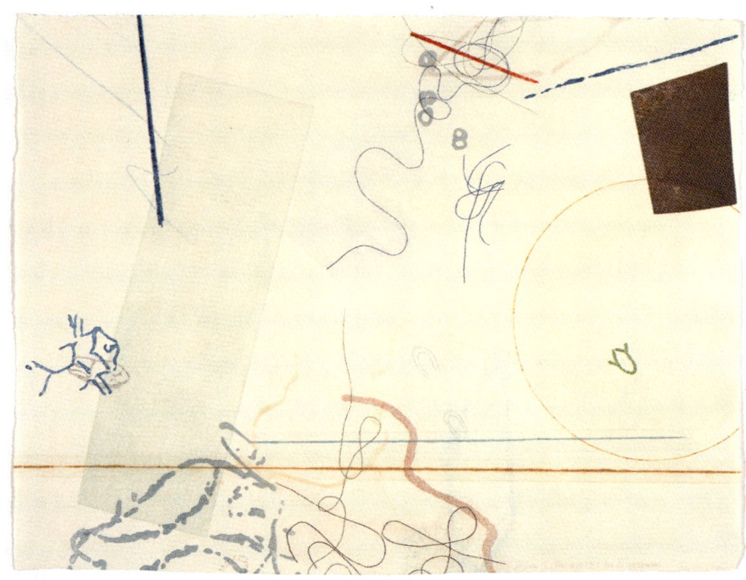

18

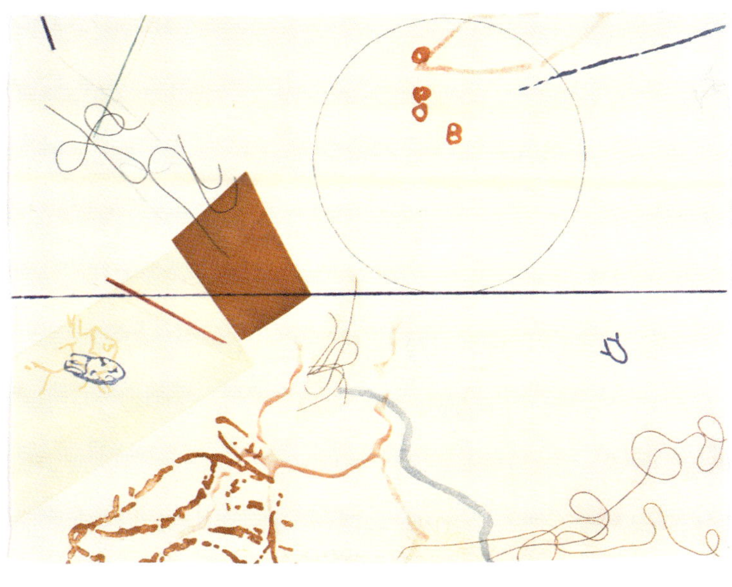

19

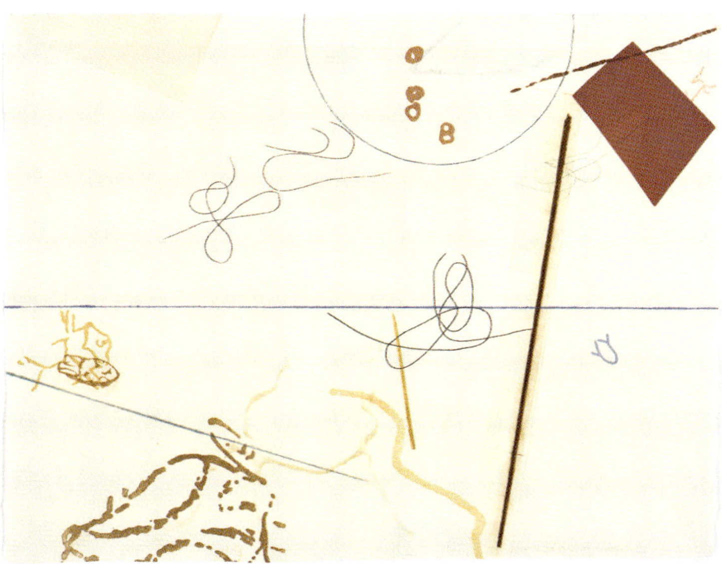

20

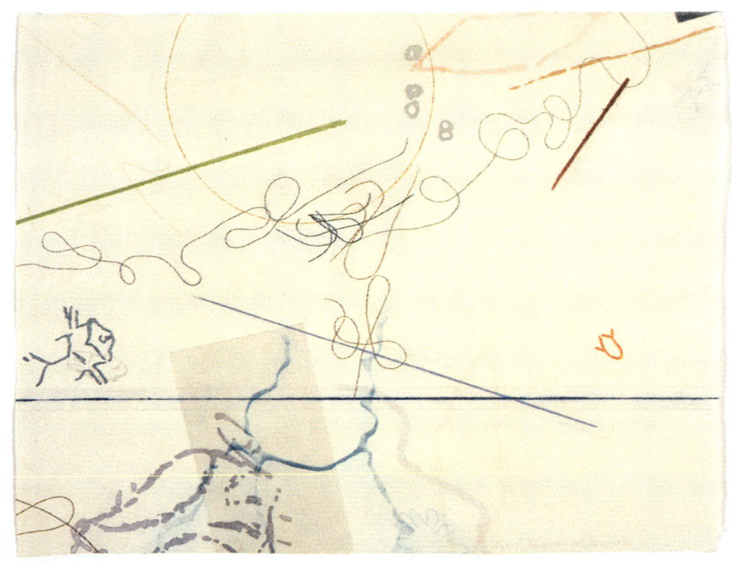

21

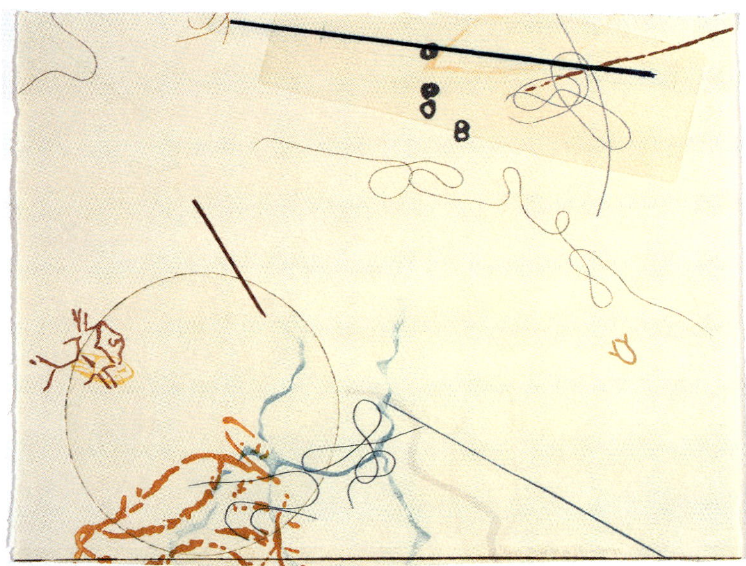

22

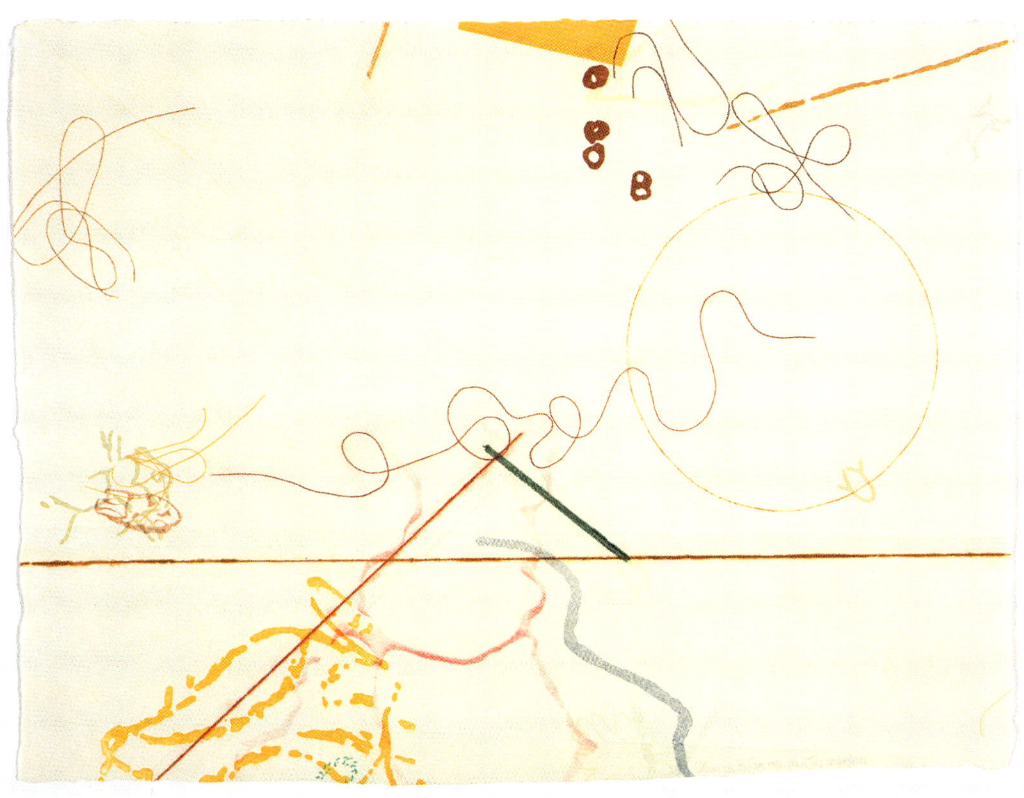

23

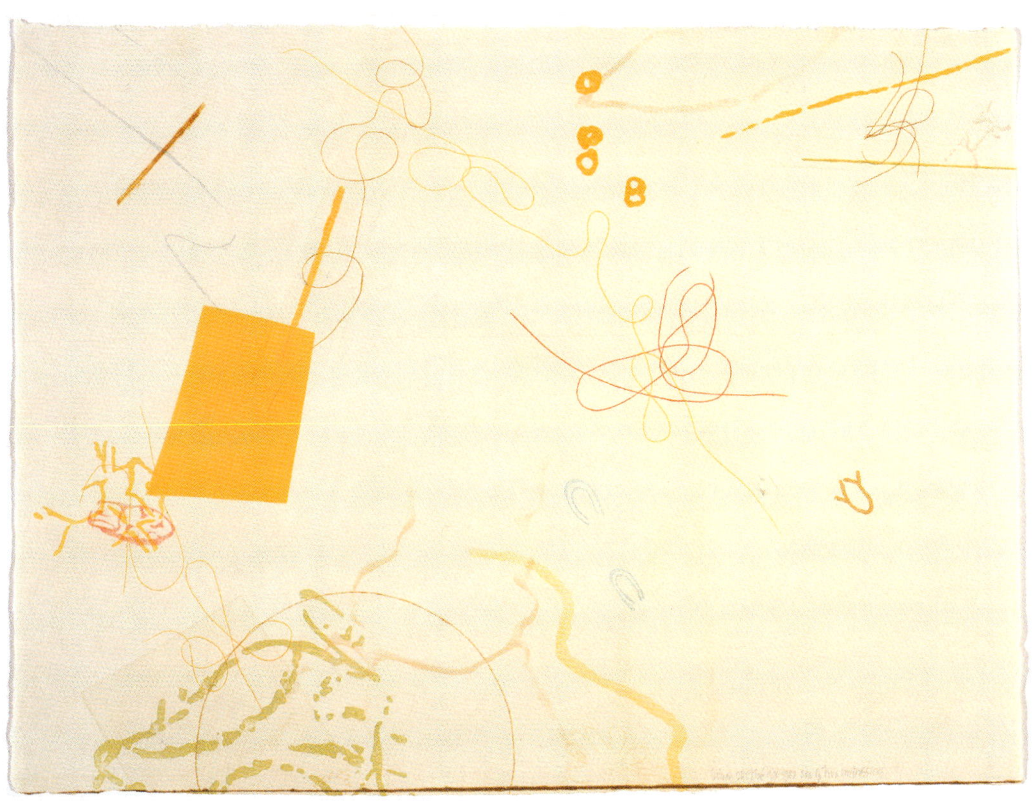

24

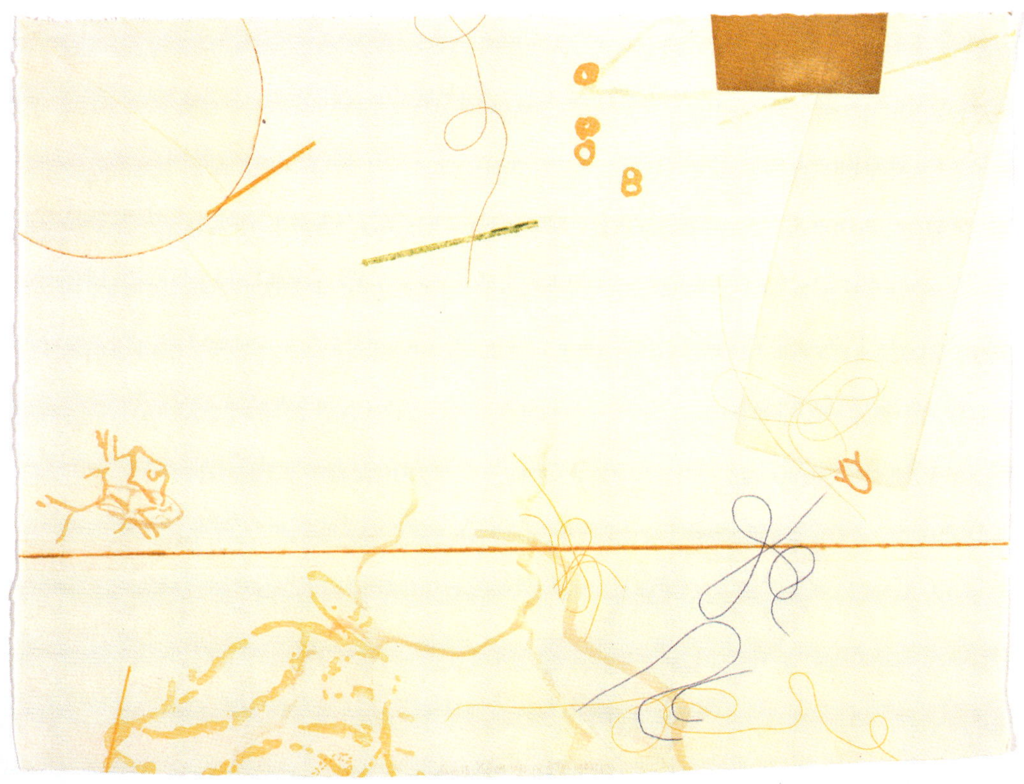

25

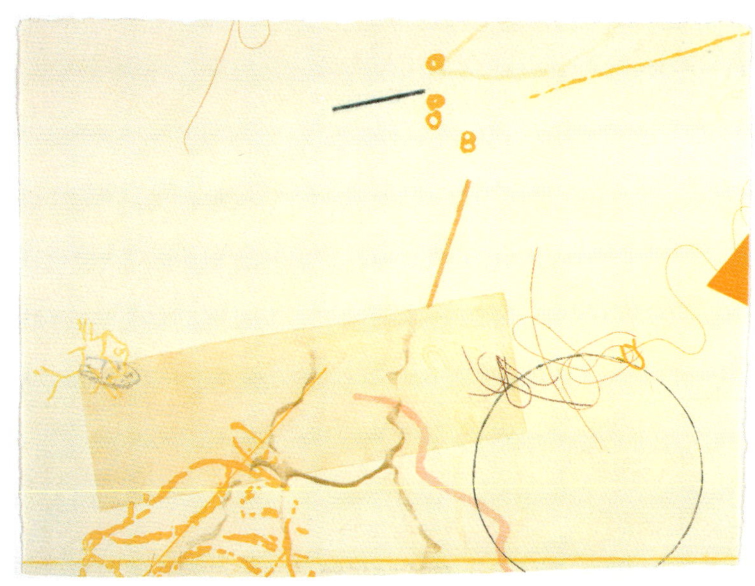

26

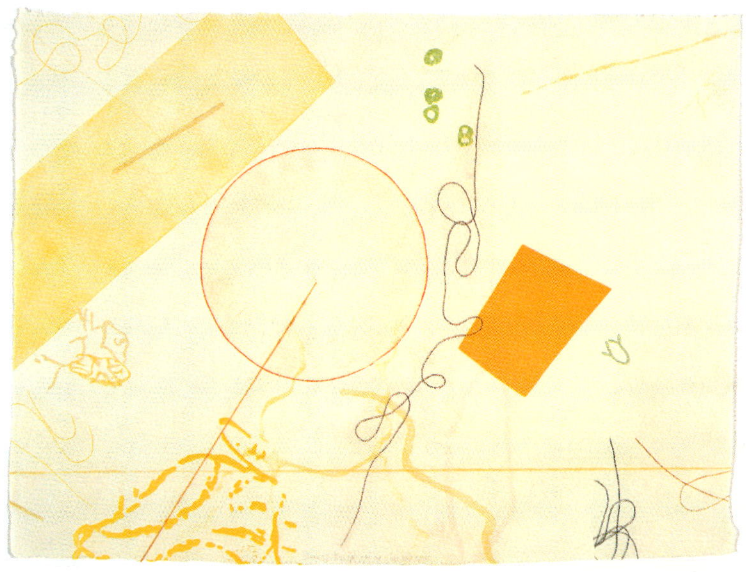

27

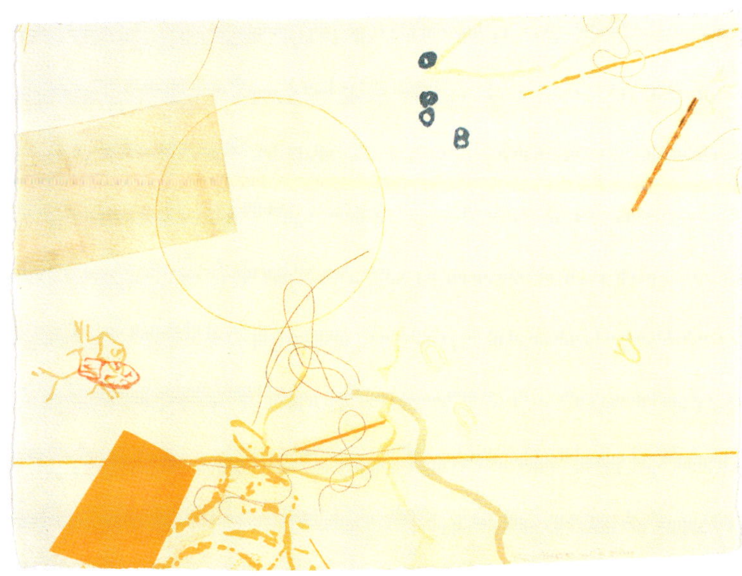

28

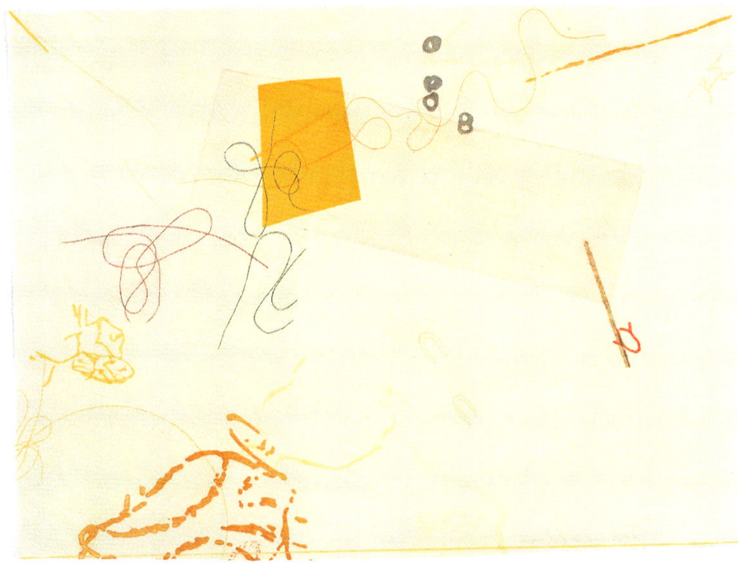

29

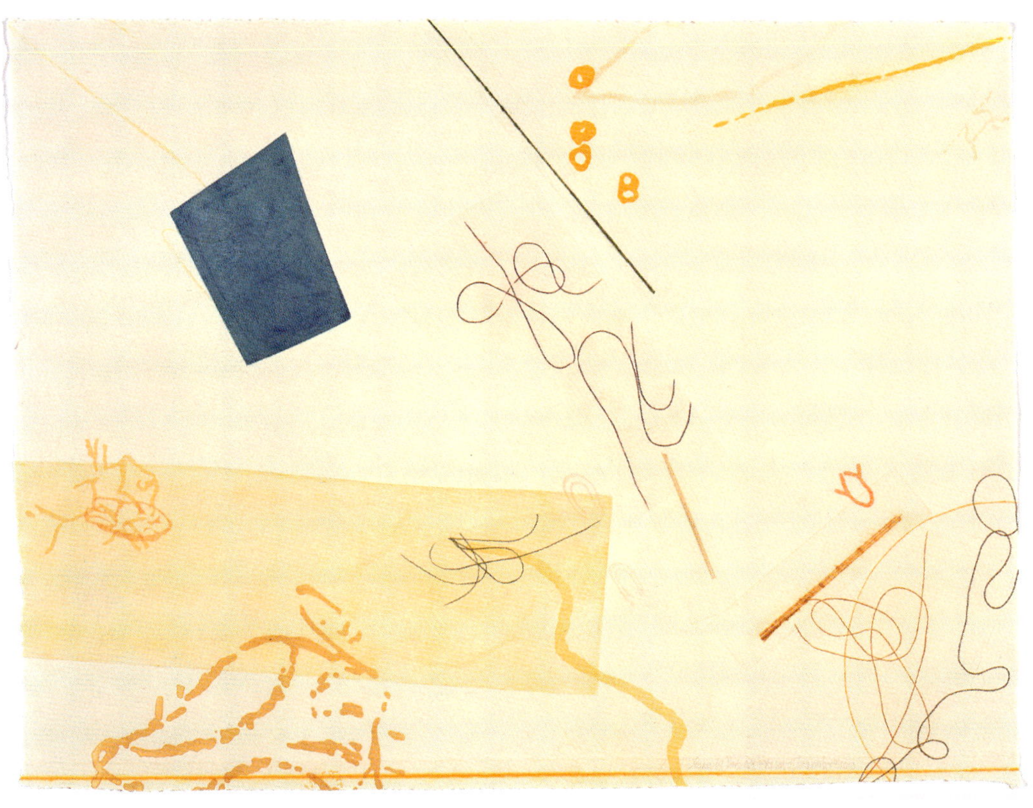

30

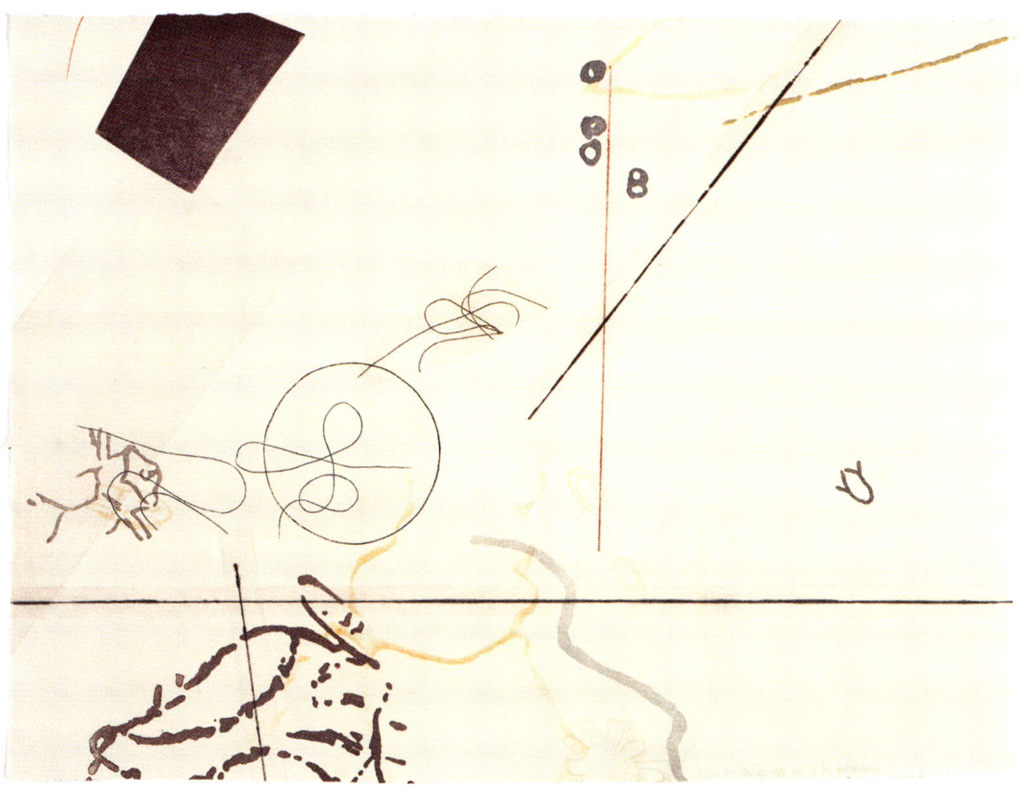

31

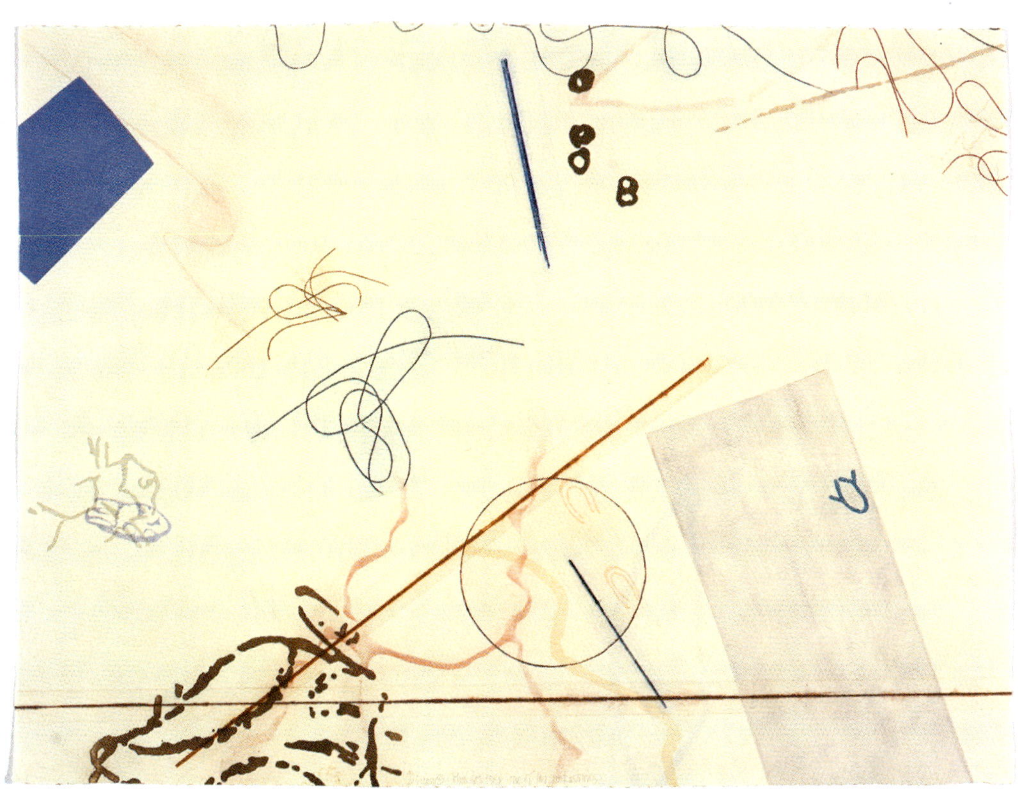

32

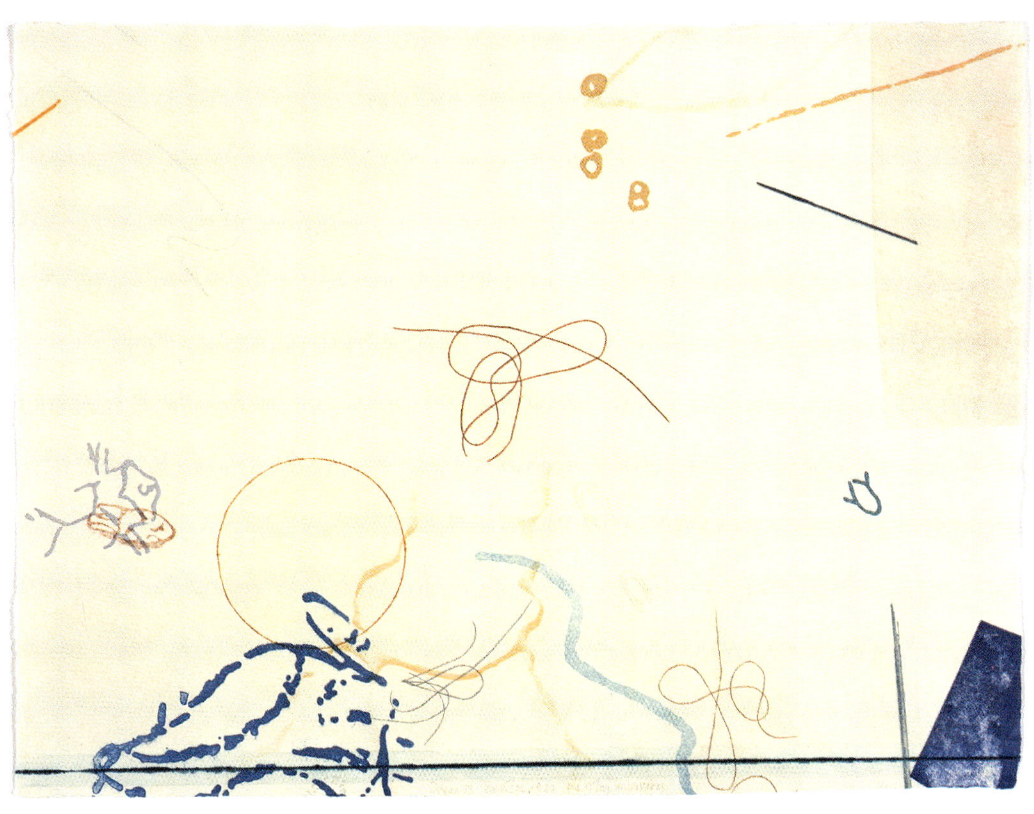

33

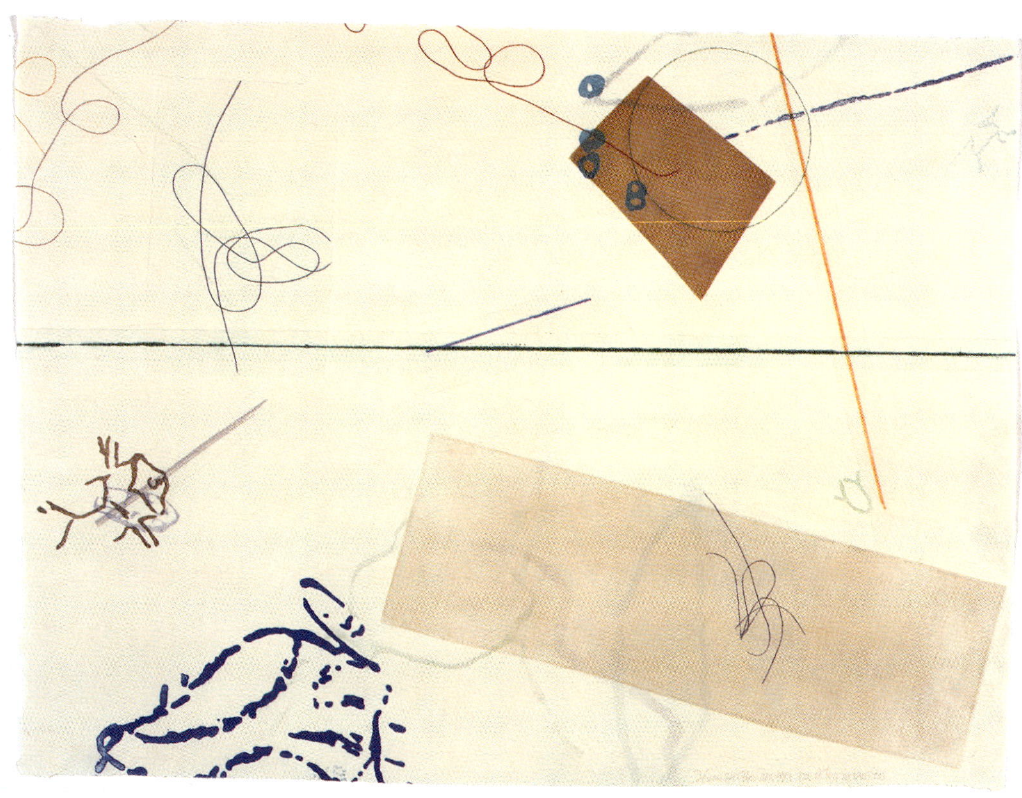

34

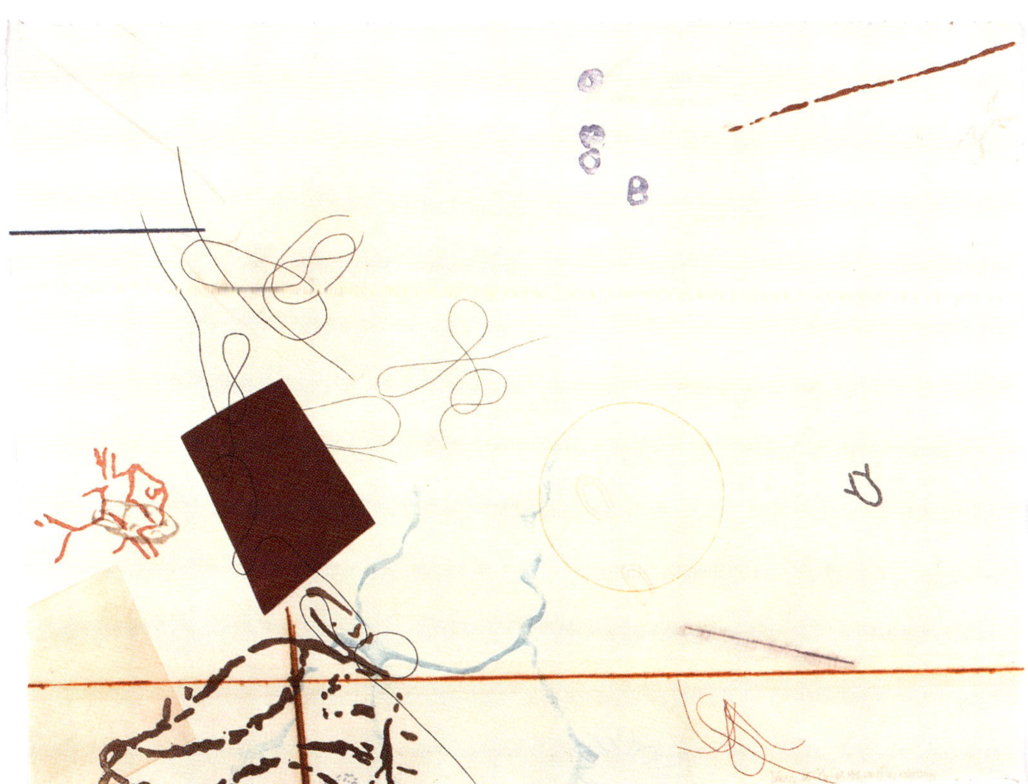

35

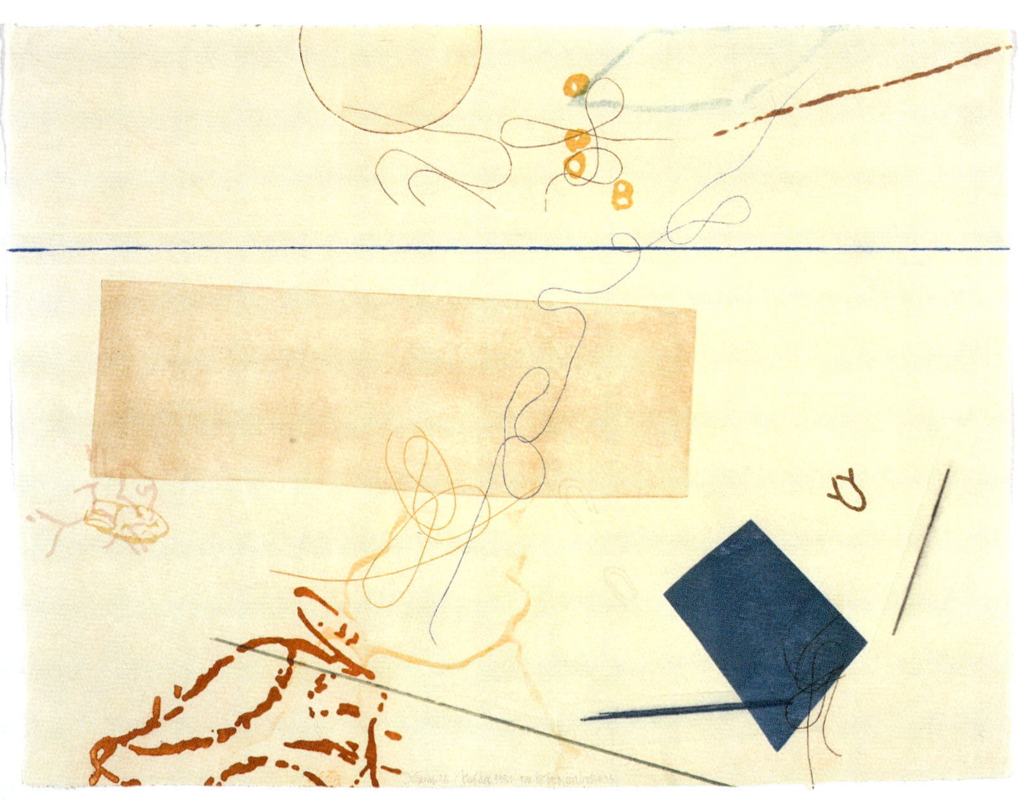

36

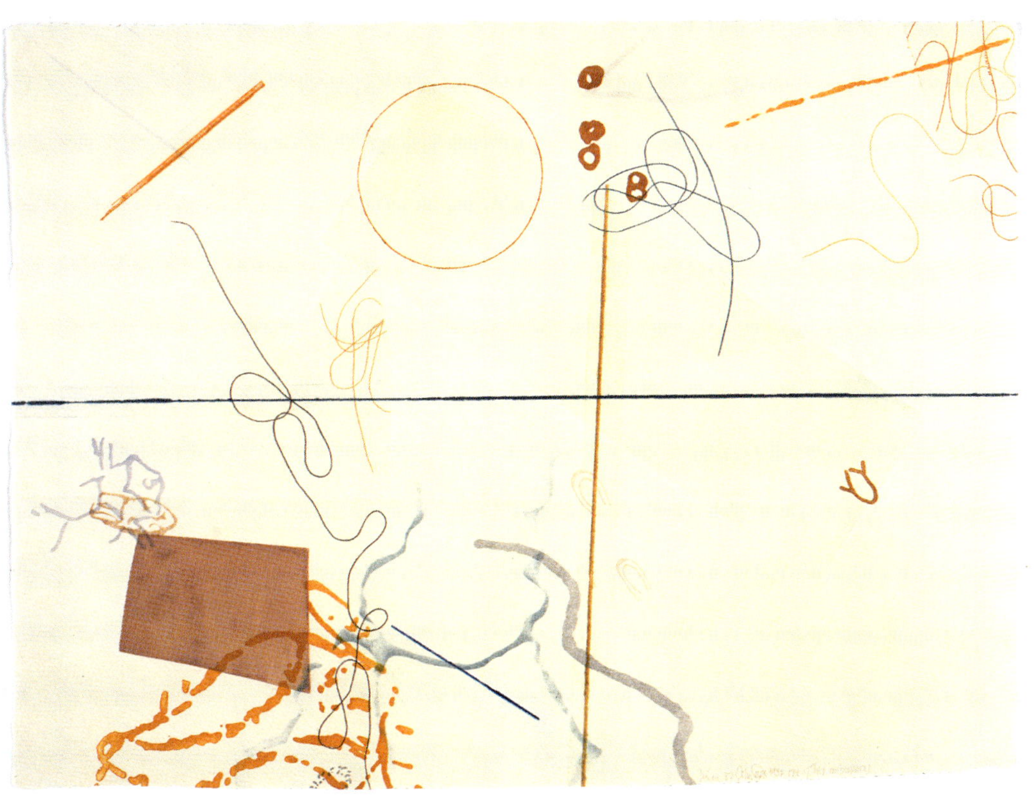

37

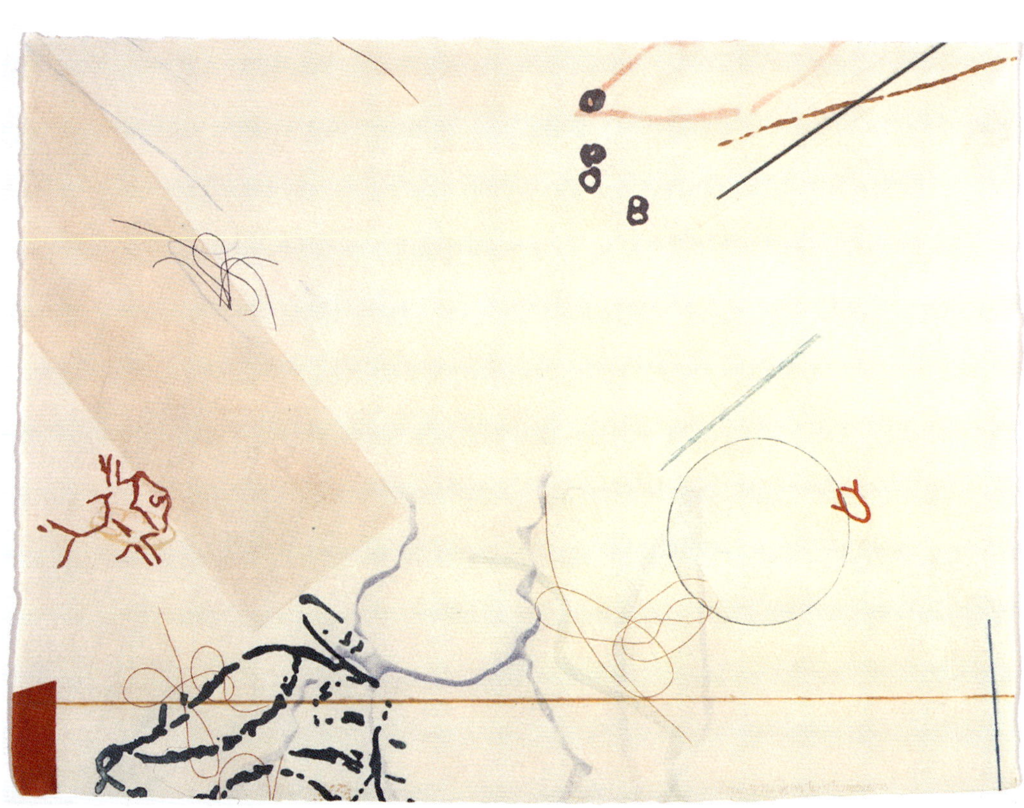

38

JOHN CAGE VISUAL ART:
To Sober And Quiet The Mind

I. BACKGROUND AND BEGINNINGS

> Art, whether it's good or bad, has a way of changing how we see the world. Oscar Wilde expressed that in one of his *bons mots*: "Nature imitates art." So you have the experience, after going to a gallery, of coming out and finding that everything you see is seen in *those* terms—the world must be transformed into *that* kind of specialness, hmm? Instead, if [seeing the art] transfers you—as Duchamp did for me—to something ordinary, then it's not as though it were a case of the "special," but it enlarges the spiritual experience to include many, many things, without giving them some kind of "dressed up" feeling, hmm?
>
> —John Cage in conversation with Joan Retallack, October 22, 1991[1]

The first thing I learned from John Cage was that the purpose of art is to sober and quiet the mind, encouraging a state that is spiritual in nature but at the same time is connected to everyday life. The notion came from his study of Indian philosophy, and he offered it to us at Crown Point Press when the printers and I had become entangled in a technical problem. He objected to our problem's being a problem. "We must be free of such concerns!" he exclaimed. "Art's purpose is to sober and quiet the mind so that it is in accord with what happens."[2]

Cage was sixty-five years old in 1977 when I invited him to come to Oakland, California, to make etchings. In reply to my invitation, he told me that he had promised the composer Arnold Schoenberg (in 1934), as a condition of studying with him, to devote his life to music. And then he added another story. He had once received an invitation from a friend to walk with her in the Himalayas, and he had not accepted. "I have always regretted this," he added. Because of that regret, he accepted my invitation and, beginning in January 1978, he worked with us for a week or two almost every year, fifteen times before his death fifteen years later.

At Crown Point Press, which is now located in San Francisco, Cage produced 27 groups of prints, mainly etchings, and the groups contain all together 667 individually composed works of art. Cage had begun his work as a visual artist in 1969 in New York with a print project, but it was nine years later, with his first Crown Point visit, that his sustained art activity began. After his introduction to etching on that first visit, he spent five years on four complex projects. Then, in 1983 he simplified his printmaking approach, and also began drawing. In the nine years after that until he died, he produced about 150 drawings at home in New York, in between regular work periods at Crown Point Press. In that period he also made 114 watercolors in two sessions at the Mountain Lake Workshop in Virginia. That is the bulk of Cage's visual art.

But there is more. He worked with others to produce several limited edition books. He worked at the Rugg Road Mill in Boston to make three suites of handmade paper using edible materials. He designed complex room-sized works of installation art on several occasions, including an installation for the Carnegie International Art Exhibition in Pittsburgh (installed in 1991 and shown in early 1992). Finally, he created *Rolywholyover: a Circus*, a traveling exhibition of his own art, along with works by other artists and a sampling of things from local museums. *Rolywholyover* was initiated by the Museum of Contemporary Art in Los Angeles and planned by Cage but realized after his death. In 1992, the last year of his life, Cage made a film[3], as well as completing his final etching project at Crown Point Press.

Cage worked with visual art in almost the same way he worked with music. His printers or assistants were something like musicians—he developed scores for them to execute. The printers were indispensable, but this was not collaborative work—the vision was his; he was the artist. You could say, however, that the circumstances of accepting invitations to work were an integral part of Cage's art production: only his pencil drawings were made independently, and they fit within a concept previously developed in his prints.

In a print studio, an artist can make art that would be impossible without techniques the printers have mastered. Many composers of music cannot play the violin but use violins in their work, and many artists who make prints cannot lay an aquatint. The composers know what a violin sounds like; the artists know what an aquatint looks like. In the course of his work, Cage grew to understand the print processes and he developed excellent skills in engraving, and in drawing with pencils and brushes. Because he worked with others, he was able to borrow some additional necessary skills.

There is one type of skill that he could not borrow or quickly learn, however, and that is skill in understanding the important issues of the art field. In this, Cage was not a novice when he began his visual work. In his youth, during the Depression years, he sold lectures on the history of music and art door to door, and studied those subjects to keep abreast of his students. Before his commitment to Schoenberg, he both painted and composed music. His friend David Sylvester has written that Cage recalled those early paintings as having been inspired by images reflected in curved surfaces; he quotes Cage as saying he used "not a brush, but steel wool, so that I was rubbing the paint onto the surface of the canvas."[4]

After Cage gave up painting, his contact with artists influenced his music. Marcel Duchamp, whom he met in 1942 and greatly admired, used elements of chance in making sculpture beginning in 1912, the year Cage was born. (When Cage pointed this out to Duchamp, he replied, "I must have been fifty years ahead of my time."[5]) Cage met Mark Tobey in 1939, and he was an influence Cage referred to over and over throughout his life. One of his favorite stories was of a painting class in which Tobey asked students to draw with noses and toes against the wall. "They all became modern artists immediately! Now that wasn't a use of chance operations, but it was a putting of the body into a situation where it could not do what it intended to do. The intention of the mind was put out of operation. And that's what chance operations do."[6]

Cage began in 1951 to use chance operations in composing his music, largely because at the time he had begun studying Asian philosophy. But one of his reasons for adopting chance as a way of working was his desire to step away from the attitudes of the Abstract Expressionist artists. He edited a one-issue art and literary magazine with Robert Motherwell in 1950, and was part of the Artists' Club where the Abstract Expressionists met. "I was with de Kooning once in a restaurant," Cage recalled in a 1978 interview. "He said, 'If I put a frame around these breadcrumbs, that isn't art.' And what I'm saying is that it is. He was saying that it wasn't, because he connects art with his activity—he connects with himself as an artist, whereas I would want art to slip out of us into the world in which we live."[7]

The idea that framing breadcrumbs might make them art was a sacrilege in the early-to-middle 1950s, but Cage had a conviction that art and life are close together. Dancer Merce Cunningham and artists Jasper Johns and Robert Rauschenberg shared his conviction, and in that period, the four saw each other almost every day. "The four-way exchanges were quite marvelous," Cage remembered. "It was the *climate* of being together that would suggest work to be done for each of us."[8] Johns and Rauschenberg are probably the most influential artists alive today, and both have spoken publicly of Cage's influence on them.

Cage talked about the "the absence of space" in Johns's work to Joan Retallack, whose interviews with him in the last three years of his life are a great treasure of first-hand information. "Something has been done almost everywhere," he said. "So it leads very much to the complexity of life. Leads us to the enjoyment of complexity."[9]

When I read that, I realized that Johns was the source of Cage's first solution whenever he got into a tough spot with his art: he would multiply the chance operations so he could fill up the page with activity. His direct debt to Rauschenberg is even clearer; a few works, especially the Plexigrams, visually resemble Rauschenberg's. Cage seems to have most appreciated in Rauschenberg's work the opposite of what he appreciated in Johns's. He spoke to Retallack of the paintings Rauschenberg made in the early 1950s that are all black or all white: "I used to have four of the white ones in my apartment down at the river. It was a marvelous experience. ...The white paintings came first, and my idea of silence came next, you know."[10]

In 1952—with Rauschenberg, Merce Cunningham, and others—Cage created the first Happening. In 1958, the highly visual score for Concert for Piano and Orchestra was exhibited at the Stable Gallery in New York. David Sylvester, in a catalog for a 1989 exhibition that included the same score, points out the visual character of Cage's scores in general, but adds that "however beautiful [a score] may be to look at, it was not made as something to be looked at."[11]

Cage's visual art, by contrast to his scores, has no purpose but the visual. In developing it, he discovered new forms. They were not a product of his will—he didn't invent them. Instead, he discovered them by opening an area of inquiry, as a scientist might do, and pushing that inquiry dispassionately to an extreme. "I always go to extremes," he once said to me, laughing.

"If you work with chance operations," he explained to Retallack, "you're basically shifting from the responsibility to choose to the responsibility to ask. People frequently ask me if I'm faithful to the answers, or if I change them because I want to. I don't change them because I want to. When I find myself in the position of someone who *would* change something—at that point I don't change it. I change myself. It's for that reason I have said that instead of self-expression, I'm involved in self-alteration."[12]

I watched Cage at work many times over many years, and I can testify that he was telling Retallack the truth. I saw him occasionally modify an approach to make it more practical to a situation, and usually he would accept an honestly made mistake, but I never saw him reject a chance-derived outcome once he had settled on a sequence of chance operations and set it in motion. Good science, also, does not modify results because of the wishes of the scientist.

There are quite a few parallels between scientific exploration and Cage's way of working, when you begin to think about it. Cage often said that he was "imitating nature in her manner of operation," for example, and I believe that scientists also do that. For some time now they have been integrating chance into their theories, and emphasizing the importance of empty space in the physical world. Even laymen like me now understand that everything in the world is made up of moving, changing particles.

Cage worked with individual units often fragmented into smaller ones, and formed them into an expanding space not limited by the traditional picture plane and not beholden to the figure/ground concerns that occupy many contemporary artists. In figure/ground thinking, the viewer chooses what to see by focusing on either a figure or its background. "I don't tend to think of a foreground and a background," Cage told his printers and me in a lunchtime conversation. "I think whatever appears does so by virtue of the emptiness of the space." [13] In Cage's work, what the viewer sees is an irregular but active stream of individual things.

Recently I discovered an article in the science section of the

New York Times that seems relevant to this. It explains that energy is "not smooth and continuous but comes in discrete packets, the quanta," and goes on to report on the work of a young researcher, Dr. Fotini Kalamara, in London. Dr. Kalamara thinks that "if we could look really close, space and space-time would turn out to be not smooth and geometrical, as in Einstein's theory, but 'bumpy' and made up of building blocks."[14] "Bumpy" is a word I will use from time to time as I describe the development of Cage's art.

I am going to use some other isolated descriptive words, too, as I continue. They are words that Cage himself put forward in *Composition in Retrospect* [15] which he wrote in 1981. He listed these ten words that he said characterized aspects of his work: *method, structure, intention, discipline, notation, indeterminacy, interpenetration, imitation, devotion,* and *circumstances.*

Someone asked a panelist at a symposium on Marcel Duchamp I attended recently why she liked Duchamp, and she replied, "Well, he's helpful." "Helpful" is also a good word for Cage's art—or you could say, more precisely, "useful." "When it's useful," Cage said in a 1978 interview, "art should spill out of just being beautiful and move over to other aspects of life so that when we're not with the art it has nevertheless influenced our actions or our responses."[16] Besides being useful in that way, Cage's art has what Rauschenberg called (in speaking of a painting of his own) the "dignity of not calling attention to itself; it can only be seen if you really look at it."[17]

The Plexigrams, 1969. Cage's first visual art project, done in 1969, was called *Not Wanting to Say Anything About Marcel*: two lithographs and a group of eight objects he called "Plexigrams," silk screen printing on Plexiglas panels. Each object consists of eight panels set into a wooden base. The panels can be reordered at will and are covered with words and dictionary-like pictures, mostly fragmented. Cage started his graphic work with *imitation*: the Plexigrams

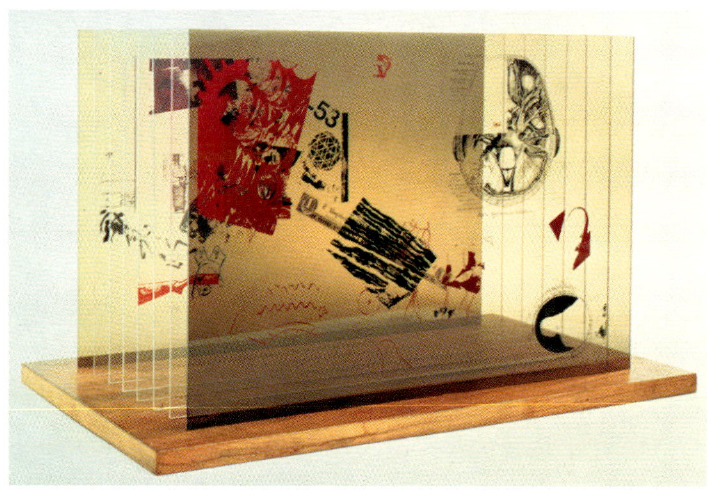

Not Wanting to Say Anything About Marcel, 1969. *John Cage with Calvin Sumsion.* **Plexigram VIII** *in a series of eight. Silk screen on Plexiglass printed in an edition of 125 at Hollander Workshop, New York City. Eight panels 14 x 20" (36 x 51 cm).*

look a lot like a Rauschenberg edition called *Shades,* 1964, and also relate to a larger mechanized work (*Revolver*) on plastic panels that Rauschenberg did in 1967. Cage's Plexigrams are different in concept, however, in that he used his rigorous chance operations to compose them.

All together there are sixty-four panels, the number of hexagrams in the *I Ching,* a manual for a three-thousand-year-old system of divination. "Chance operations" is a specific term that Cage used to describe a method of working in which he used numbers derived from the *I Ching* to provide him with ways to proceed. He would use a series of numbers resulting from throwing three coins six times to answer questions of yes or no, how many, and this or that. To compose the Plexigrams, he asked whether words found in the Random House dictionary should be fragmented before appearing in the art, and whether they should change into images. If images were asked for, Cage used the dictionary illustration if there was one. Otherwise, he selected the picture by using chance operations on images from the New York Public Library Picture Collection of the World.

Every operation in Cage's work process was discrete, with coin-throwing for each tiny step. Carl Solway, who with Alice Weston published the Plexigrams, reports that among the receipts for bills paid is one to an assistant for throwing coins. Irwin Hollander at the Hollander Workshop in New York did the printing, and Calvin Sumsion, whom Cage invited to participate, did the paste-up of the images in preparation for transferring them to silk screens. "I composed the graphic work and he executed it, just as I would write a piece for a pianist and she would play it, or he would play it," Cage explained. "In other words, in moving from music to graphic work, I took with me the social habits of musicians, hmm? The division of labor, so to speak."[18]

Not Wanting to Say Anything About Marcel, 1969. **Lithograph B** *in a set of two. Lithograph printed in an edition of 125 by Irwin Hollander at Hollander Workshop, New York City. 27-1/2 x 40" (70 x 102 cm).*

We can see *intention* in the Plexigrams. Cage intended to make a work of visual art using procedures he had established for writing music. In fact, looking back on his visual art as a whole, it seems to me that he always started projects with intention. Then, for the details, he put the "intention of the mind out of operation"[19] by using *indeterminacy,* or chance operations.

After the Plexigrams were completed, Cage made two lithographs by selecting panels by chance operations from the first four Plexigrams for Lithograph A and the second for Lithograph B. Solway told me that after asking the printers to proof the lithographs on white, gray, and black paper, Cage simply chose the black paper for the prints.

Much later, Cage summed up the project in this way: "The important thing I think in this is that Marcel died. And that the way I chose to not say anything about that was to use the dictionary, to subject it to chance operations, and then to let the words die, hmm? To let them die in the Plexigrams and in the black paper."[20]

From my point of view, the most important aspect of the Plexigrams is the *method* Cage devised for placing images on a page. He laid a grid over the page, then asked the *I Ching* for coordinates on it. After locating an image on the grid at those coordinates, he would turn it against a protractor to the number of degrees specified by chance operations. He used this method, with or without the protractor, for most of his graphic works and some of his music over the rest of his life.

II. A MUSICAL APPROACH

I'd like to know if you ever think in images and if so if you ever use visual thinking as a source for your work with sound? When I first went to Seattle, my friends took me to a small aquarium in the market. When you got in, there were just these boxes of water. ...After a while a clam went up from the bottom of one of the tanks to the top and then having gotten some air sailed back down. When he arrived at the bottom, that disturbed others and they went up and shortly it was a magnificent display.

I thought of that when I was at the Crown Point Press one January and I was going to make some prints. I decided to make a series called *On the Surface.* I placed [etching plates] at chance-determined points and...when they crossed the surface at the top I [cut the plates]. The work began with large shapes and ended after 35 prints with very small shapes.

I enjoyed that work so much that when I had the project of a piece for orchestra I decided to do it the same way, to...put templates at chance determined points on the music paper. Then I noticed that whereas for the etching the top of the paper was important and going down was interesting, for music going up and going down were not interesting. What was interesting about music was going from the left to the right. And so I had to change the direction and the meaning of the chance operations.

—John Cage responding to a questioner at Harvard University in conjunction with The Norton Lectures, 1988.[21]

The First Crown Point Prints, January, 1978. We began our first project with John Cage at Crown Point Press on a holiday, January first, because it was necessary for him to leave on January 8 to fulfill another commitment. He flew to Oakland, where our studio was located at the time, from New York on New Year's Eve.

He brought with him a score that, "was the door that opened from music, for me, back into the field of graphic—paying attention to how things are to look at."[22] He had written Score (40 Drawings by Thoreau) and 23 Parts: 12 Haiku almost four years earlier.

In the score there are twelve bars each divided with vertical lines into three parts of five, seven, and five equal divisions, like the syllables of a Haiku poem. The lines control duration for the performers. In composing the score, Cage had overlaid the lines with images sketched by Henry David Thoreau at Walden Pond in the margins of his *Journals*; the images are the same size as they appear in the Dover edition. Each musician performing this work receives one of twenty-three parts into which the drawings are fragmented. Cage had brought us the conductor's score in which the images appear whole, the score without parts.

Using the score as a model, he made the etching titled *Score Without Parts (40 Drawings by Thoreau): 12 Haiku.* Cage traced some of Thoreau's drawings onto the plates, and copied some freehand, using different chance-decided etching and engraving techniques. The little pictures of a skunk, a squirrel, an eddy in a pond were his introduction to our world: hard ground, soft ground, drypoint, and engraving.

"I had the sense that I was not an artist, that I couldn't draw, really, anything; but that I had done this [score] and it would make an etching, and did," he said fourteen years later. "From now," he added, "I would say not a very interesting one but, nevertheless, something. And then I made a rather interesting thing there, which was the *Seven Day Diary.* ... Since I couldn't draw, I decided to close my eyes and draw. ...And if I dropped my tool someone would put it back in my

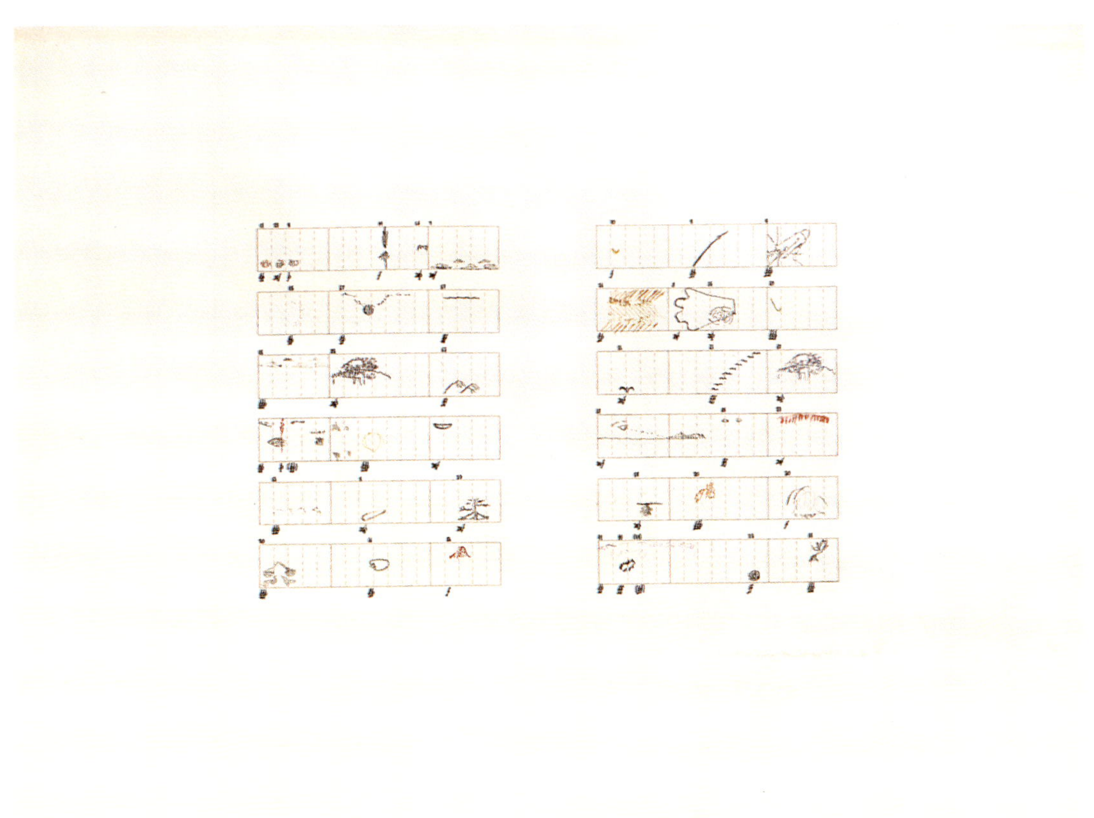

Score Without Parts (40 Drawings by Thoreau): Twelve Haiku, 1978. *Etching with drypoint, engraving, aquatint, and photoetching. Printed by Stephen Thomas in an edition of 25 at Crown Point Press. 13 x 18" (33 x 46 cm) on 22 x 30" (55 x 77 cm) sheet.*

1

2

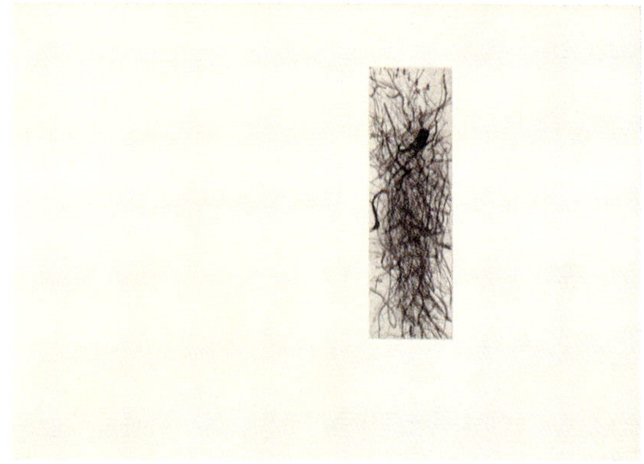

3

4

5

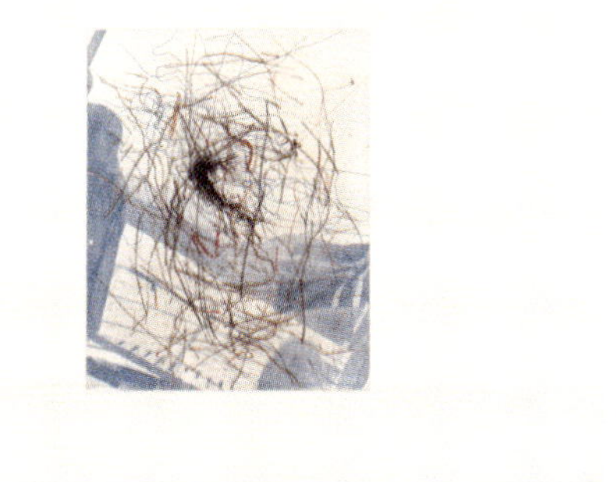

6

Seven Day Diary (Not Knowing), 1978.
Seven etchings with drypoint, aquatint, and photoetching in a portfolio. Printed in an edition of 25 by Stephen Thomas at Crown Point Press. Sheet size 12 x 17" (31 x 43 cm). Plate sizes vary.

7

hand for me. I was surrounded by helpers."[23]

As he did in most of his projects at Crown Point, Cage started *Seven Day Diary* with what he called "the first thing," the paper. He chose one he liked from the ones we had. Each day, he chose a plate size by chance operations and oriented it on the paper using the method he had developed for the Plexigrams.

The first day he used the first two techniques that we would teach any student, drypoint and hard ground etching. (He did a test with just one and found it too skimpy.) He numbered the different tools and asked which to use, then how many marks to make with each tool. Next he asked how many marks should be long, how many medium, how many short. He had with him a sheaf of pages showing *I Ching*-derived numbers, computer-printed and ready to use to get answers without the need to throw coins.

Each day we added a new technique. In this project, however, he couldn't use engraving, a technique he had especially liked in *Score Without Parts*, because engraving requires full attention: you must push the tool through the copper rather than drawing in the normal way.

Cage began his work at Crown Point Press, as he had his work on the Plexigrams, with *intention*. This intention involved *notation*. *Score Without Parts* is his only graphic work that uses music notation. *Seven Day Diary*, which followed *Score Without Parts*, focused on *method,* and also on *interpenetration*: lines long, medium, and short piled up and mingled with one another.

***Signals*, 1978**. Perhaps it was signing prints from the previous working time—thirty-five (the edition plus artist's proofs) of each image, all alike—that led Cage to the idea of making plates and printing them only once. Perhaps he was thinking, after he left us in January, that it was a shame to throw away the Thoreau photo transparencies, and that led him to the notion that whoever ultimately owned the print should own the plate and everything else connected with the print's making. He didn't say so at the time, but I think he enjoyed engraving and wanted to see if he could learn to do it well. Probably those factors and some others shaped the intention behind the *Signals* project. In any case, during eleven days in September 1978, we made 35 prints, and we pulled only one impression of each. The prints were dispersed along with their plates, maps, drawings, notes, etc., to individual purchasers.

Here is the structure: There are three elements—Thoreau drawings, circles, and straight lines. Although images can overlap, each one is an individual, with its own color and its own size, the colors and sizes chosen by chance operations. Many of the Thoreau drawings are enlarged and partly fall off the plates, which Cage thought of as nets that probably would catch images but might not.

Two prints in the series did not catch images of any kind and are blank. Cage asked us to ink them anyway, and he was delighted with the film of ink—the hand tone—and the occasional faint scratches that printed. "I'm producing a situation like what happens in nature," he explained to us. "Certain things happen, and then because of the concatenation, sometimes nothing results."[24] Cage engraved the straight lines, and allowed the possibility of many of them attached to one another, each new one changing direction. It was an ambitious set-up for a beginner, especially since this type of line shows every tremor of the hand, every lapse of attention. Joan Retallack asked him, in remembering this project, if "you found yourself, despite your usual proclivities to the contrary, developing a skill?"

"Yes," he replied, "it's quite exciting to be able to do that. To make a long line from scratch, so to speak. ...I remember offering Jasper Johns one of my prints, one of my etchings, and he chose one in which I had slipped. I said, Why did you choose that one rather than the other? And he said, Because you slipped."

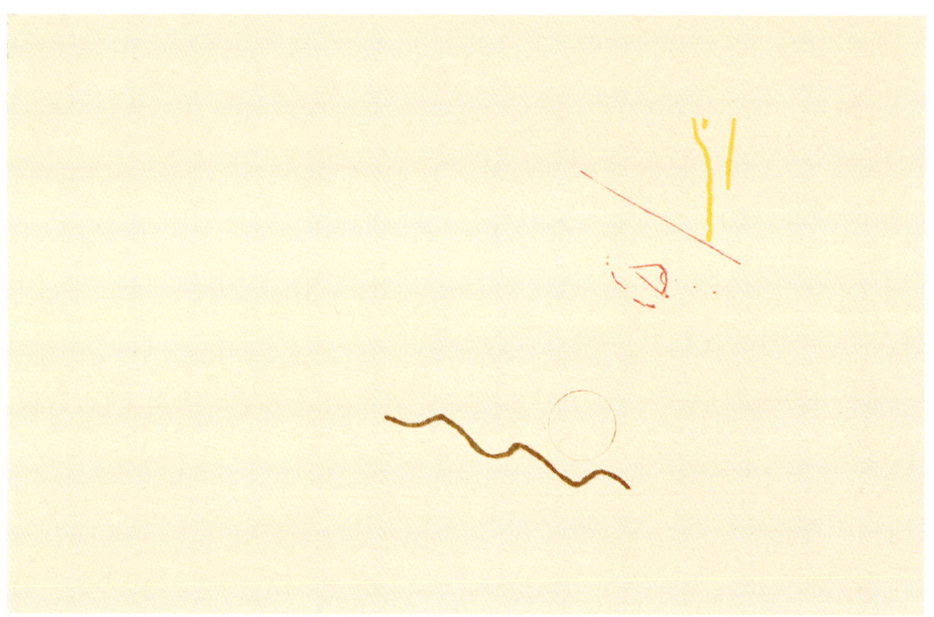

Signals, Artist's Proof 5, 1978. *Unique impression, one in a series of 36 related prints. Printed by Lilah Toland at Crown Point Press. 8 x 12" (33 x 51 cm) on 13 x 20" (20 x 30 cm) sheet.*

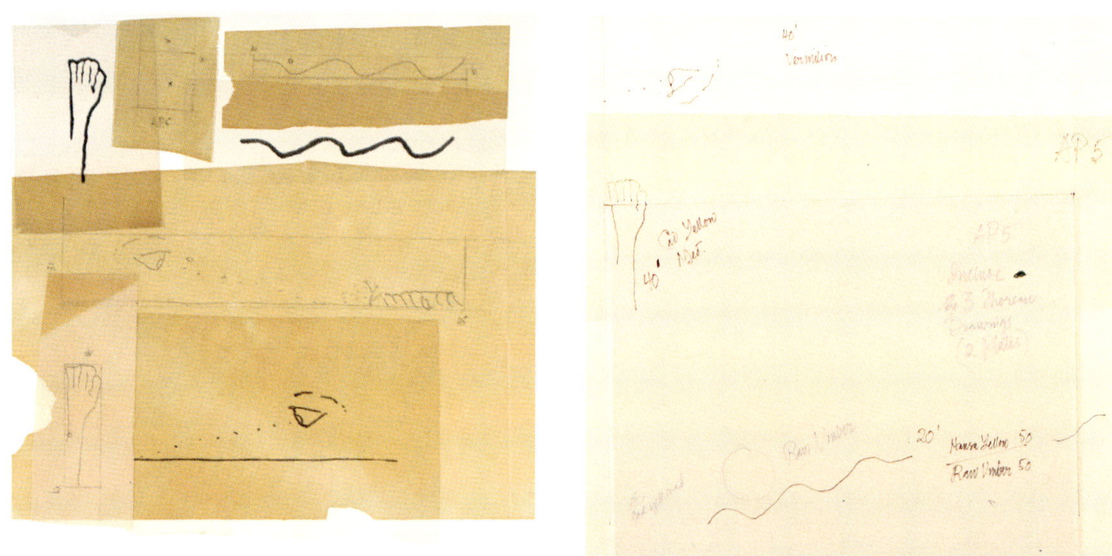

Working drawings and photographic transparencies for **Signals AP 5**. *In this series, only one print of each image was made, and the working material and copper printing plates remain with the print.*

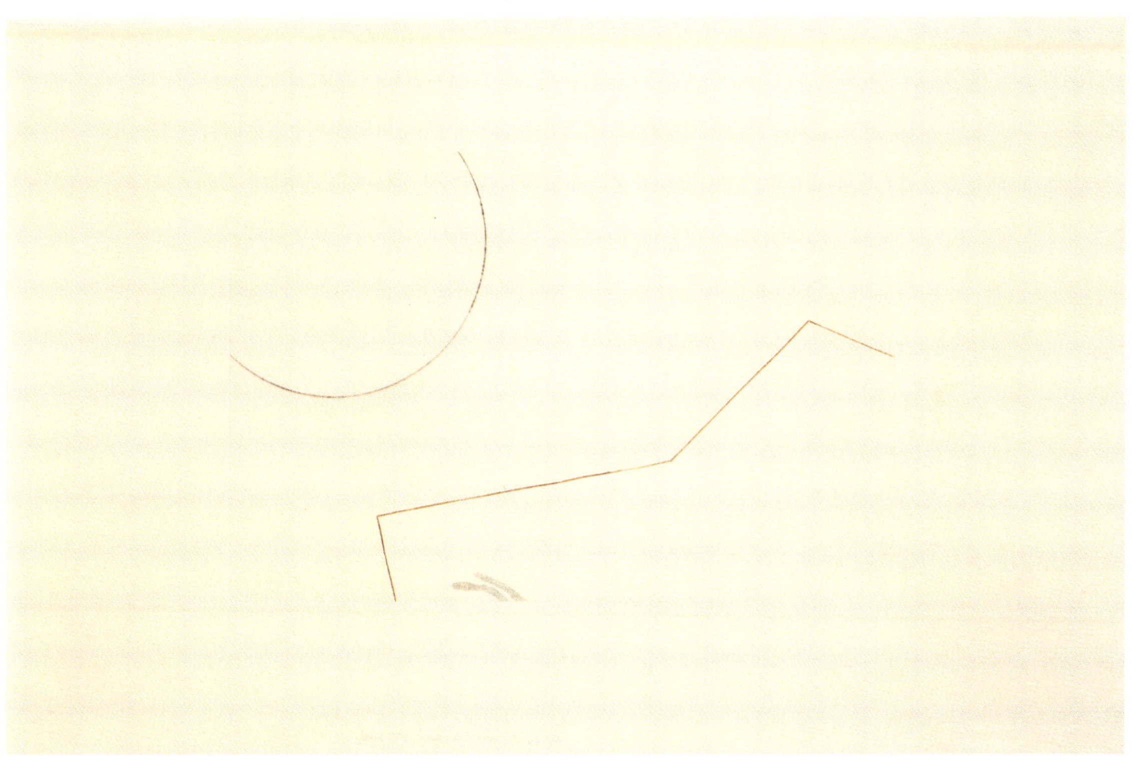

Signals 23, 1978. *Unique impression. In this print the score indicates that there should be nine straight engraved lines. But only four lines are visible, the others having disappeared off the plate edges. (You can see the plate mark as a dented line.)*

CHANCE OPERATIONS. In this book, whenever I use the term "chance operations," I am using it, as Cage did, specifically to refer to his use of the Chinese *Book of Changes,* or *I Ching,* as a mechanism for making chance-determined selections among various options that he would define. Indeterminacy, which simply means that there is an indefinite number of solutions to a particular problem, was at the heart of all Cage's work, and using chance operations was his preferred way of creating indeterminacy. But he had other, simpler ways as well. Dropping a string to find the path of a line, for example, was a way of using indeterminacy without using chance operations.

On several occasions, I heard Cage tell the story of a classroom exercise conducted in the 1940s by his teacher, Arnold Schoenberg. Schoenberg sent the students to the blackboard with a problem and asked them to turn around when they had a solution. Cage turned around, and Schoenberg asked for another solution. This was repeated several times, until Cage said, "There are no more solutions," and Schoenberg then asked for the principle underlying all the solutions. The students that day were unable to find that principle, but Cage discovered it much later in life. The principle underlying all the solutions, he told us, was the question that was asked.

In using chance operations, Cage began by formulating questions. In a 1978 interview for a Crown Point Press publication, he explained this clearly: "Most people who believe that I'm interested in chance don't realize that I use chance as a discipline. They think I use it—I don't know—as a way of giving up making choices. But my choices consist in choosing what questions to ask."[25] He usually would come to the studio with an idea, and his questions had to do with practical ways to explore it using the materials and methods available. He enjoyed having a very large pool of possible answers, so there would be an indefinite number available, and his complex system of chance operations using the *I Ching* provided that.

The *I Ching* is an ancient book of wisdom still used by many people. Cage used it strictly to generate numbers that he would then employ to find answers to the questions he asked in order to form his work. The earliest recorded explanation of the use of the *I Ching* is by Confucius, writing in the sixth century B. C. E., but the book itself is probably older. It consists of 64 hexagrams, each of which has a number and a name. The practice of consulting the *I Ching* has many time-honored methods and varied possibilities for interpretation. But, in general, you begin by constructing a hexagram of six lines, some solid and some broken, one above another, drawn starting at the bottom. You throw three coins to get each line. If you throw two tails and one head you draw a solid line, two heads and one tail a

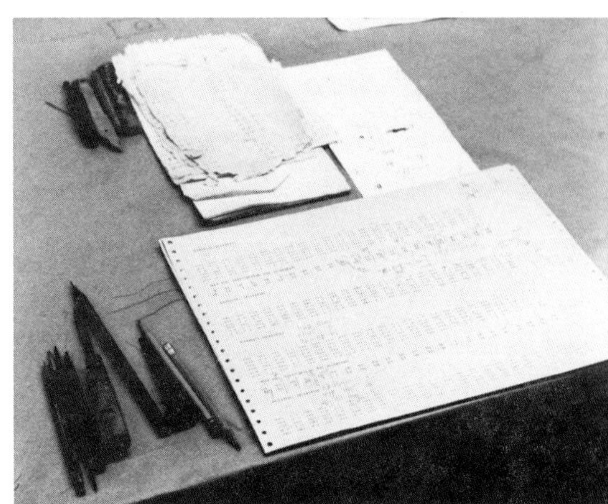

A 1978 photograph of Cage's worktable showing tools, computer sheets, and equivalency tables used for Seven Day Diary.

broken one. If you throw three heads, you draw a solid line with an O in it to indicate that it can change; three tails makes for a broken line with an X to indicate its changing, or moving, nature. If you have any moving lines in your completed hexagram, you immediately draw a related but changed hexagram in which each moving line becomes its opposite: a solid moving line becomes a fixed broken one and a broken moving line is fixed and solid.

In Cage's computer printout illustrated here, solid lines are shown as three dashes, broken ones as two. Notice that the moving lines are indicated, and the changed hexagrams are also shown. The numbers listed in the "Key to Identifying the Hexagram" are the ones you would find if you drew those particular hexagrams and looked them up in the *I Ching.* I looked up the top left stack of lines and found it to be Hexagram Number 31, *Sensing,* changing to Number 33, *Withdrawal.* And sure enough, the first two numbers in the key are 31 and 33 (read from bottom up). Since the next hexagram in the row did not change, the next pair of numbers are both 52, the hexagram called *Mountain.* If you were using the *I Ching* for wisdom, you would think about your situation in terms of *Sensing* and then *Withdrawal* if you had received the first pair of hexagrams, or *Mountain* if you had received the second. You would be able to obtain further (and even more diffuse) advice from texts that accompany each hexagram as well. I am giving you this information as background and to demonstrate the simplicity and the accuracy of the computer program. Cage ignored the hexagrams and their meanings and went straight for the numbers; he needed a lot of them. Until 1967 when his music work HPSCHD engendered the program, which was written for him, Cage had done a great deal of coin-throwing. The program was a time-saver. It did not compose his work for him, but it generated the *I Ching*–derived numbers he needed for his system of chance operations.

The printout shown here is one of the pages Cage used when he was working on the print series *Seven Day Diary*. In composing *Seven Day Diary,* each day Cage added a new etching technique. He numbered all the tools that could be used for that technique and his first question was which of them he should use. Probably for the bit of work we're concentrating on, the number 33 gave him his tool. But I am sure there were not 33 tools available—you can see the tools on the table in the photo; there are about a dozen. The number must have been adapted somehow. Moving on, we can read Cage's handwriting on the printout and see that he assigned the tool 31 lines, and that he broke the 31 into three unequal parts so some lines would be short, some medium, and some long. I didn't see where he got the numbers he used as breaking points, so I asked Andrew Culver, who later programmed Cage's own computer at his home, and he figured it out. The breaking points, Culver says, are derived from the numbers 9 and 41, which Cage adapted by using equivalency tables that you can see in a pile above the printout on the worktable in the picture. He also used the equivalency tables to turn the too-large number (it must have been 33 or 52) into one of the actual number of tools available.

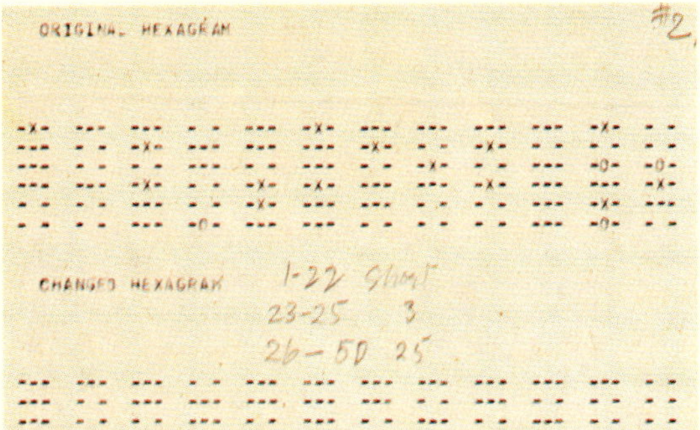

Part of the computer printout shown at left.

Culver pointed out that formulating questions was only the first step for Cage in using chance operations. The next one was formulating ways to answer the questions using the numbers provided. There are 64 hexagrams, so his choices always ran from one to 64. He answered questions of This? or That?, for example, by treating the numbers one to thirty-one as This and thirty-two to sixty-four as That.

In his handwritten equivalency tables, Cage had broken the number 64 into two, three, four, and up to 63 parts and they enabled him to make the kinds of conversions we have been discussing. He carried the tables with him everywhere and had thumbed through them so much that their edges were ragged. Culver later set up Cage's computer to produce what he called "IC Supply Sheets," tables of *I Ching*–derived numbers already adapted into equivalency tables. After that, Cage used them for his chance operations and no longer needed to carry with him the printouts and dog-eared tables that you see here.

Cage's primary reason for using chance in forming his art was to get away from his own taste, so he never drew things in a particular way, chose particular colors, or put images in particular places simply because they looked good to him. Having said that, I'll ask you to thumb through this book and see if you agree with me that everything does look good. How could he be so lucky, someone asked me, if he didn't care what his work looked like? The answer is, of course, that he did care what his work looked like, as do all visual artists. His originality, the reason *we* care about his art, is in his discovery of a way to tap into (you could say) the music of the spheres.

Cage's artworks are vast, and even if we see a whole one together (as we do in this book with *Déreau* and *HV2*), we have the feeling that there could easily be more parts. Each work consists of a large open-ended group of individual smaller works that themselves are made up of confederations of images and marks. It is conventional to use the word "series" to describe related works of art, and I have used it in relation to Cage's prints, but it is not an accurate designation; no member of a group necessarily follows from another. However, the members of a group clearly belong together. They are linked by Cage's choices in setting up an arena in which chance would participate in their making.

Each time he began a new project, we would do tests so Cage could see what parameters to set. How many lines should be allowed? Up to 64? Or up to 5? Or 3? If the test results showed no magic, he might reduce the number—more often he would increase it. But once the parameters were in place, no matter what appeared, he would accept it.

LOCATING IMAGES. Cage's work essentially is about individuals appearing together in a space, so there is nothing more important to the form of the art than the location of images. Cage located individual images in relationship to the whole, rather than to one another. But once they were located, relationships among them developed—usually these would change within the scope of the entire work.

In order to place images into a space defined by a sheet of paper, Cage began with a grid the size of the paper. Since his location practice was tied to his *I Ching* chance operations, and in the *I Ching* the number 64 defines everything, his grids were divided into 64 parts horizontally and 64 vertically. Shown here is the grid Cage used for *Changes and Disappearances.* He used a protractor in composing this work, so we have placed one on the grid so you can see what it looks like.

In *Changes and Disappearances,* Cage made many small shaped plates, and their images float across the page. He numbered each plate on its reverse and determined (using chance operations) a corner to be labeled A, then continued marking the corners clockwise around the plate with B, C, and D as needed. He then asked the *I Ching* for two numbers and two adjacent letters, 7–26 and BC, for example. He covered the grid with a piece of tracing paper (he could see the gridlines through it), and—in the example given—marked the spot where vertical gridline 7 crossed horizontal gridline 26. He put the plate down on the tracing paper with corner B resting at the marked spot. Then, he set the protractor on top of the plate, with its central point at corner B, and rotated the plate under the protractor until side BC lined up with a specific angle. In the example we are using, the first plate listed in the score for Print 16, the angle was 120 degrees. Once the plate was located, Cage traced it on the paper.

Shown on this page is an equivalency table Cage wrote out to adapt his *I Ching* numbers for use with the 360 degrees of the protractor. As you can see by his long division sum at the top of the page, he began by dividing 360 into 64 groups. He found out in this way that 40 of his groups of numbers would have six members, and 24 would have five. Andrew Culver helped me figure this out. He guessed that the reason Cage formed the groups of five at the beginning and end of the table, with the groups of six in the center, was that he liked symmetry. Culver said that he once asked Cage what he though of symmetry, and Cage replied that it was good, "because it meant no bias." In order to get to the 120 degrees in our example, Cage must have received the number 22 from the *I Ching.* With that number, his table narrowed the answer down to six choices, 115 through 120. To select one of the six, he asked for another number and converted it to the sixth choice, 120, by consulting one of his regular equivalency tables, the one that broke 64 into 6 parts.

I have been describing the way Cage located the plates within the framework of the paper in the *Changes and Disappearances* project, but there was another sort of locating going on as well. That was the location of each image on each plate. Each plate had one curved side, which Cage obtained by dropping an inked piece of string onto the copper, then cutting with a jig saw over the mark left there. The additional (straight) sides—how many and how long—were defined by chance operations. Once all the plates had been made, Cage set about the process of locating images on them. The process was ongoing throughout the printing of the series.

There are three types of images in *Changes and Disappearances:* straight lines, which Cage drew on the plates with drypoint; curved lines, which he engraved over marks made by dropped strings; and images from the diary of Henry David Thoreau, which we applied photographically in the darkroom. I am not sure how Cage determined the placement and length of the drypoint lines, but it is clear that he had made a rule that the lines should not be drawn over one another (where lines cross in the prints, it is caused by plates overlapping). In the darkroom, each Thoreau image was

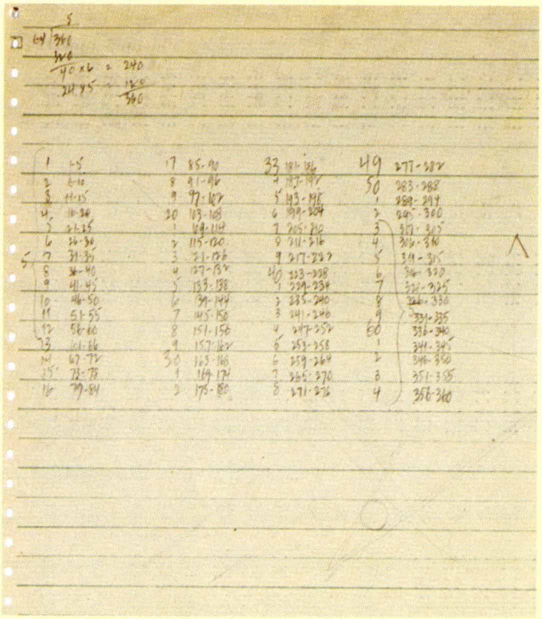

A page of Cage's notes showing tables for adapting the protractor to the I Ching. *Sketched on the same sheet are some plates of the type used for* Changes and Disappearances.

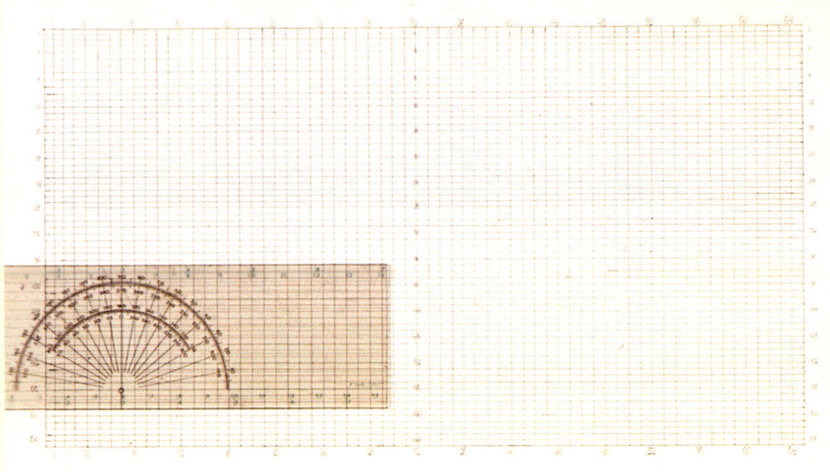

Cage's grid for Changes and Disappearances *shown with a protractor used for locating images. The grid is the size of the paper on which the series is printed .*

located by setting the plate (or a template matching it) on the table of an enlarger in a chance-determined place, then projecting the image from a chance-determined height through a chance-determined lens opening. Thoreau's nature images became very abstract. Sometimes they would "disappear," in that they would fall entirely off the small plate. In fact, the title of this work was originally simply *Changes,* but Cage added the word "disappearances" after we began the work in the darkroom.

Most of the disappearances that took place, however, were in the printing process, not in the darkroom, and they were only temporary. After Cage had put images (Thoreau drawings or his own lines) on the plates, in any particular print there was a possibility that they might fall outside the borders of the paper. If the protractor was located so its central point was near the edge of the grid, turning a plate against it might result in part of the plate sticking out beyond the paper as the print ran through the press. The images were still there, but the paper did not catch them. This corresponded to Cage's often-repeated comment that "music is continuous—only listening is intermittent," or "art is everywhere; it's only seeing which stops now and then."[26]

MAPS AND SCORES. As Cage located one plate after another, he added their tracings one by one to his sheet of tracing paper. If he had already drawn a plate in a spot specified for a new plate, in *Changes and Disappearances* he would move to another sheet. After all the plates for a print had been located, his series of tracing paper maps were used to register the plates in printing.

The printers first traced a copy of Cage's grid on long-wearing Mylar, and taped it to the bed of the press. On top of this, they fastened the first map, which Cage had labeled Run 1, using tape on the two top corners and aligning tic marks Cage had made with the corners of the grid. After inking all the plates for Run 1 the printers positioned them by slipping them under the map, and then adjusting (if necessary) their places on the grid by checking Cage's score, the written record of his chance-derived instructions. When ready to print, they removed the map and laid down a sheet of printing paper. After running it through the press, they fastened one side to the bed so it would stay in register, then removed the plates, put the map for the next run in place, set the next group of plates on the grid, and ran the press again. The plates in each new run printed on top of the previous ones. The printers continued in this way until all the runs were completed and the print was made. Then, for a second print they inked the plates again and started over with the registration. We made only two or three impressions of each print.

As Cage applied his chance operations, he preserved the results of his *I Ching* consultations in what he called scores. Sometimes he made a series score, sometimes separate scores for each individual print, sometimes both. In *Changes and Disappearances* we have both: the series score was concerned with making the plates, and the individual scores were concerned with positioning, inking, and printing them. Apart from the series score, Cage made an individual score and a set of five or more maps for each print.

AN INDIVIDUAL SCORE. Shown here are the score for Print 16 of *Changes and Disappearances,* and the map for Run 1. If you turn the page, you can find the rest of the maps for Print 16 and a small reproduction of it. Since printing reverses images from the way they are drawn, we show this study reproduction reversed. You can easily compare it to the maps. Print 16, correctly oriented, is shown in a larger size on page 81.

Below the score, we have numbered the columns to make them easy to refer to. **Column 1** gives the identifying numbers of the plates that appear in this print. There are 22. Cage made 66 plates for the series by cutting eight copper plates the size of the paper into chance-determined shapes. The most plates used in any print turned out to be 45, the fewest 13. After all the 35 prints in the series were made, one plate had never been selected to appear.

Column 2 gives the coordinates on Cage's paper-sized grid that he used to locate the plate in the print. **Column 3** gives two letters identifying the edge of the plate to be placed on a particular angle of a protractor. **Column 4** gives that angle. You may recognize the figures in the first line of the score, the ones for plate 56, as those that I used as examples when I explained how Cage located plates in this series.

Column 5 is titled "Edges Inked." Cage had noticed in earlier projects that the printers carefully cleaned the edges of each plate before printing to be sure no ink was clinging there, and he decided to reverse this and ink some of the plate edges. The pairs of letters in this column indicate which edges should be inked.

Column 6 gives the colors for inking the edges. The colors listed were mixed to obtain the color used—all the specified edges of a plate were inked in the same color. In planning the way colors were formulated in the *Changes and Disappearances* prints, Cage started with the unusual gray-blue tone of the paper, and decided that each color would have at least ten percent blue. You can see the blues listed in the first part of the formula: ultramarine, cerulean, thalo, indigo, and so on. For each color listed, he asked his *I Ching* chance operations if it should be pure blue (there were seven pure blues available), or blue plus white, or blue plus another color (twenty-four other colors were available), or blue plus another color plus white. The printers mixed individual colors for the edges of each plate, and also for each image on each plate that was used in a print.

Column 7 shows in which press run that plate is included and also on which map it can be found.

Column 8 gives the particular color mixture for each mark on each plate. Plate 56, shown on the top line of the score, is the small triangular plate you can see on the left side in the map for Run 1. Despite its small size, it has ten marks; Cage has written out the colors for each one both in the score and on the map. The line labeled 1, for example, is 80 percent ultramarine blue and 20 percent Lilah gray (the Lilah colors, named after printer Lilah Toland, are brown or gray, and are mixtures of everything left over after the other colors are mixed). Line number 2 is thalo blue with fi white added. Number 3 is 50–50 thalo and veridian green with 1/10 white and so on.

1 2 3 4 5 6 7 8

Score for Changes and Disappearances 16 *(shown on page 81).*

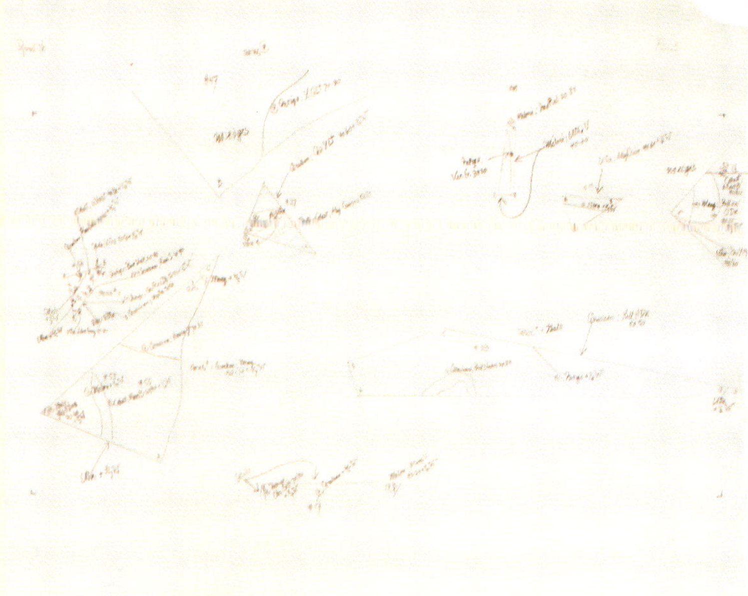

Map for Print 16, Changes and Disappearances, Run 1.

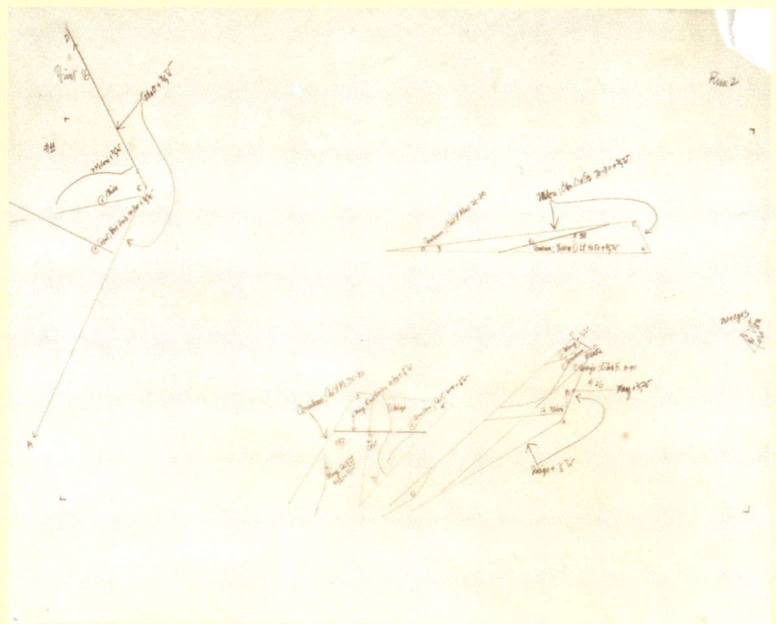

Run 2

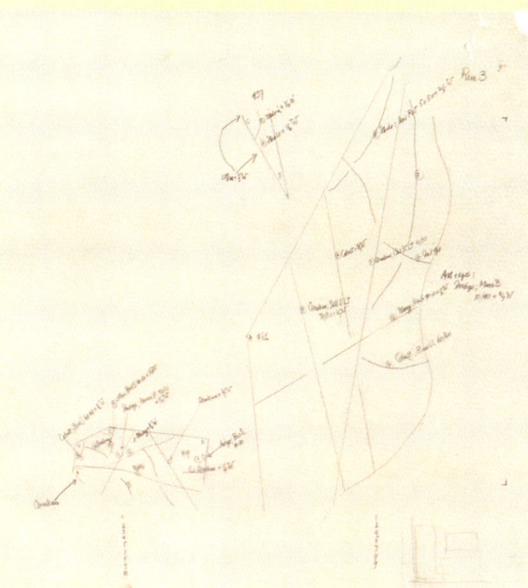

Run 3

On this page you can compare the images in the maps with their counterparts in the print. The irregularly dotted lines, whether they are straight or curved, are plate edges that have been inked. The thick fuzzy straight lines are drypoint. Cage drew them with a sharp tool that pulled up a burr of metal; the burr holds ink and creates the soft character of the line. The wiry curved lines are engravings, which Cage made with great skill by pushing a tool (faceted so it removes the burr) through the metal over the images of strings he had dropped on the plates.

The key idea behind the *Changes and Disappearances* prints is that members of a pool of individual plates appear and reappear in the different prints, and each time a plate appears, there is the possibility that it will change irrevocably. After determining through chance operations that a plate would appear, Cage asked another question: would it change? If so, he asked whether he should add a drypoint line or an engraving. Having added the line, he assigned it a color mixture, as he did each line already on the plate. As the series progressed, the plates became more complex.

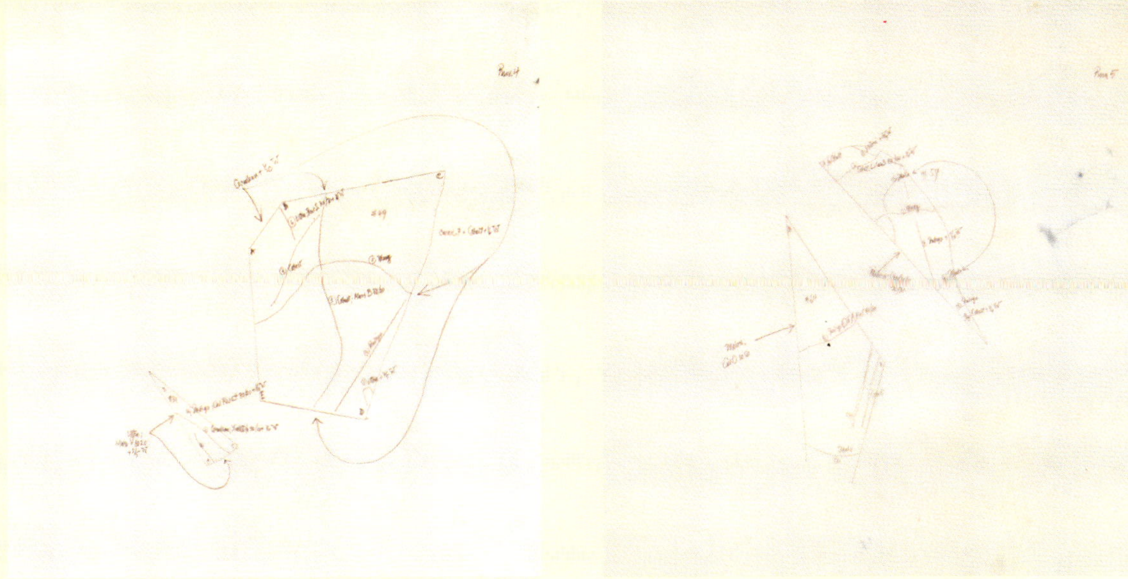

Run 4

Run 5

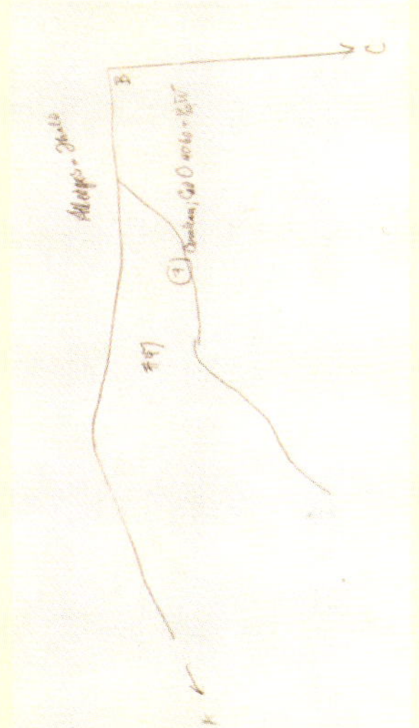

Run 6

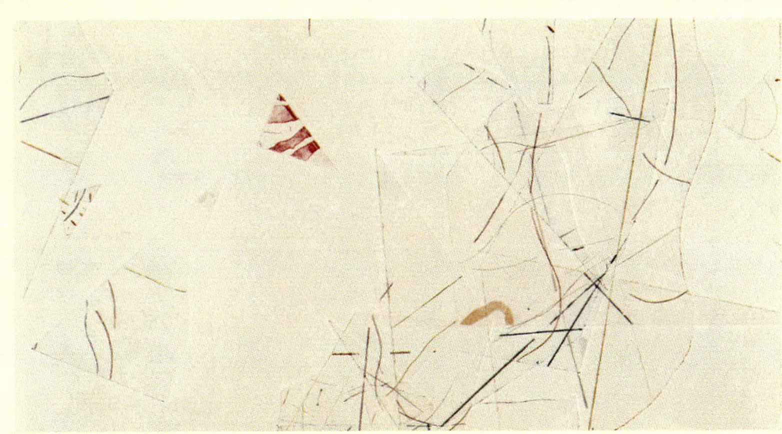

Changes and Disappearances 16, *reversed.*

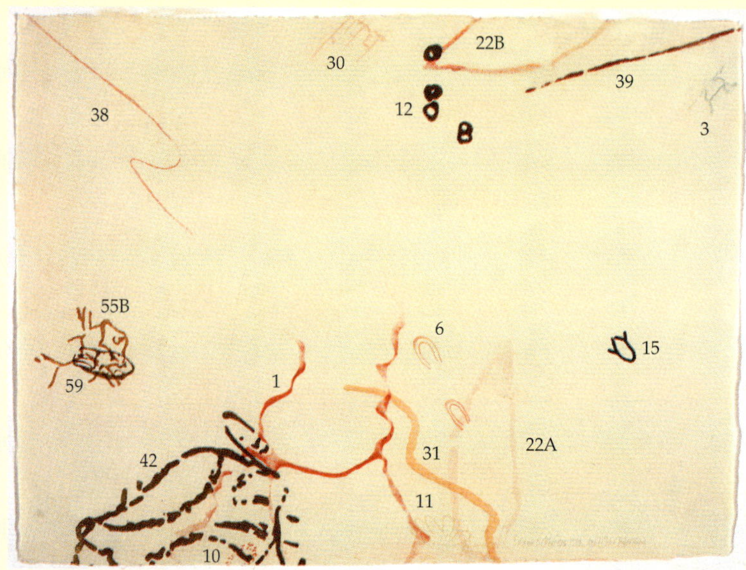

Key to the Fixed Images, a modification of Déreau 5.

THE MAPS AND SCORES FOR *DÉREAU*. *Déreau* is the set of prints illustrated at the beginning of this book. Its title combines the words "décor" and "Thoreau." Cage's earlier large sets of prints, *Changes and Disappearances* and *On the Surface,* had centered on changing groups of individuals caught in various configurations in a space defined by the paper. In this work, the third and last big set, the drawings of Henry David Thoreau integrate with the paper to form a frame for the activities of the other images. The Thoreau drawings are fixed in place. They are the décor, or the scenery, on the stage that is the paper. The actors—or dancers—that move through the scenery were themselves originally Thoreau drawings, but they "disappeared" and Cage reincarnated them as different kinds of marks, all of which are mobile.

He began by using chance operations to choose 24 of the hundreds of drawings Thoreau had sketched in his *Journal.* I do not know how he created the pool (probably 64) from which he selected this group. After selecting the drawings, Cage and the printers took negatives of them into our darkroom and set up a group of photographic variables—lens opening, exposure, etc.—that Cage had prescribed in his series score for the prints. Then, following the score, they made positive transparencies to use in transferring the images to printing plates. In this process, 12 of the 24 Thoreau drawings disappeared. I have illustrated the score on page 75 and will discuss it in detail, but first let's look at the Thoreau drawings that did not disappear (the fixed images) and the figures (the mobile images) that Cage substituted for the ones that did.

Shown here is something I've called a Key to the Fixed Images. It is a print of *Déreau* from which we have removed the images that are mobile. On the facing page is a map that Cage drew that shows the mobile images separately from the fixed ones. The numbers in both illustrations correspond to the image numbers in Cage's score.

By studying the **Key to the Fixed Images** you will be able to see all the Thoreau drawings that were on the plates—in the prints, a few of them come and go. They were all inked and printed every time, but different colors were used in each print, and some of the images are so faint they do not show in all colors. We chose Print 5 for this exercise because it is the only print in which we have been able to find Image 30. This image is especially lightly etched into the plate.

The **map** we have reproduced here is the second one Cage drew, the one for Print 2, and it shows his excitement in beginning a new project. The *Déreau* maps differ from the ones Cage made for *Changes and Disappearances* in that for *Déreau* he did not include the Thoreau images or the color mixtures on the maps, and he drew only one map for each print, combining the different runs on a single page. In both series, Cage made the maps to record the locations of the plates after he had conducted chance operations to discover where they would appear on the paper. The printers used the maps to locate the plates on the press bed. In drawing the

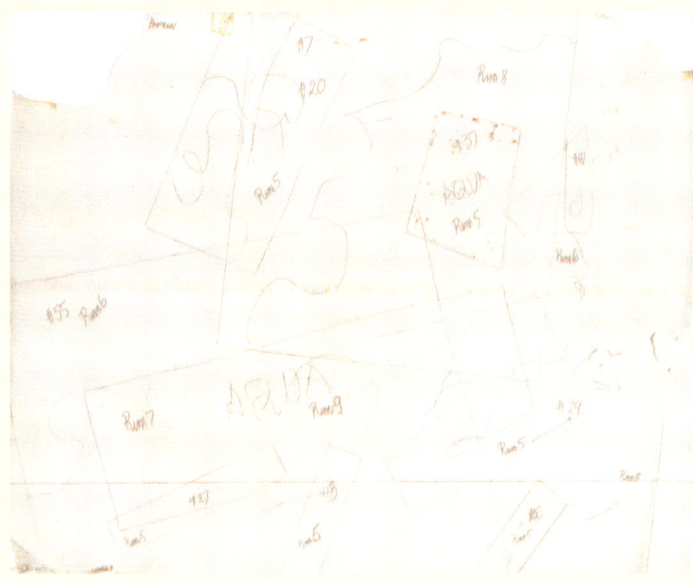

Map for the Mobile Images, Déreau 2.

maps, Cage traced the plate images and labeled them with information that the printers needed.

The twelve **mobile images** are substitutions for the twelve Thoreau drawings that disappeared during the darkroom operations, and they retain the identifying numbers of the original drawings. The mobile images have characters that are quite different from the Thoreau drawings, however, and also they are different from one another.

The first mobile image is a **horizon line**. It moves freely up and down on the page. Cage drew with drypoint a straight deep line across a narrow plate the width of the paper, and used this plate in every print. The second is a **circle**. Cage divided the prints in *Déreau* into ten groups, and he made a new circle for each group—actually he made nine circles; one is repeated. He cut circular plates out of pieces of copper. The printers inked the unmarked surfaces of the plates and left ink on the edges, so there is a very light veil of tone on each circle and a somewhat dotted line around it.

You could say the horizon and the circle are the stars of the show, and the other ten mobile images are the supporting cast. There are **three bars**, **five strings**, and **two aquatints**. Cage made the **bars** by drawing a chance-determined number of drypoint lines close together so each set of lines creates the impression that it is a thick line, or a bar. He made 30 plates with bars on them, three new ones for each of the ten groups of prints. He did not make new string plates for each group, however. He engraved five **strings** and used all of them in all the prints. He used a yard length of string for each one, and asked the *I Ching* whether he should drop it in the center of the plate, making a concentrated image, or along the edge, making an expansive one. Each string plate was the same size and shape as the photographic transparency on which the original Thoreau drawing was processed in the darkroom at the time that it disappeared.

Cage also made two **aquatints** the size and shape of the transparencies for the replaced Thoreau drawings. The aquatints create relatively flat fields of color, and are both used in every print. Their presence is visually a strong one. Their densities and whether or not they are even in tone were determined by chance operations—one is transparent, the other opaque, and both are uneven. They print more or less smoothly depending on their colors. This was the first time Cage had incorporated aquatints for their own sake into a work, although from the beginning we had used them to provide tone in the photographically etched Thoreau drawings. Using aquatints to create wide passages of tone provided a new visual element for him, and you can see that he took pleasure in that: he wrote the word "aqua" prominently in the early map we have reproduced.

THE SERIES SCORE for *Déreau* is shown on page 75. We have added numbers to the columns so I can refer to them. The heading "24 Drawings by Thoreau" probably was the first title and demonstrates Cage's concept that all the elements in the prints are Thoreau drawings, though some of them are changed.

In **Column 1** Cage listed the individual numbers of the 24 selected Thoreau drawings. Four came up twice in his chance operations and are repeated, so there are 28 lines in the score. If a drawing was repeated, Cage added B to its number (sometimes he went back and marked the other one as A, sometimes not).

Column 2 is the mystery column. With the help of Lilah Toland, who printed *Déreau* eighteen years ago, and Leo Holub, who is a professional photographer, I have arrived at explanations for most of the material in the score, but Column 2 continues to stump us. There are symbols (dots, check marks, X's, and what look like infinity signs) and Cage wrote "disappeared" after images 55 and 41. Why did he write "disappeared" next to only two images? He made it clear in other ways that twelve Thoreau drawings disappeared. Perhaps he simply neglected to label the other ten, but possibly there is something different about these two. Holub does not think the symbols relate to the darkroom work, so I am assuming they relate to the images generally, and I wonder if they concern the disappearances. The ten Thoreau drawings that disappeared but are not marked "disappeared" are marked with a check mark and an X. The two that Cage labeled "disappeared" are marked instead with a dot and an infinity sign, a pair of symbols that otherwise accompany the Thoreau images that did *not* disappear. And, looking outside the column to another mystery that might be related, what about the legend at the top of the score that says: "No Record of [infinity] positions on grid"?

Whenever I get tangled up with something like this, a little voice comes into my head that says, "If you think of it that way, you won't know what to do. What is the *first* thing you do?" That voice is Cage speaking to our printers when they got bogged down with his chance-derived instructions. Clearly, this column is not the first thing to think about. Let's move on.

Columns 3, 4, 5, and 6 concern the work done in the darkroom. Cage prescribed the listed photographic variables in advance using chance operations and, when the printers executed them, some images showed up weakly or not at all. Those were the ones that "disappeared." Cage and the printers made positive film transparencies of the images that made a strong appearance, and later Cage used his chance operations with a grid to locate those images on plates that we could etch and print. We had previously covered the plates with a light-sensitive, acid-resistant emulsion, and after the positives were in place, we exposed the plates to a strong light that hardened the emulsion where the light got to it. Then we washed away the emulsion in the image-areas. Cage didn't subject the exposure time in this part of the sequence of events to chance, because the timing had to be exact or the emulsion would not harden and all the images would fail.

At Crown Point at the time, we had two lenses for our enlarger, 50-millimeter and 135-millimeter. **Column 3** shows which lens Cage assigned to each image. Normally, you would use a 50-millimeter lens with a 35-millimeter negative and a 135-millimeter lens with a 4 x 5 negative. We think the negatives were 4 x 5, so where a 50-millimeter lens was used, only the central part of the image would have been projected faithfully and a fading out would occur at the edges. This is visible in the print, for example, in Image One, the large swirl at the bottom.

I am unsure of the meaning of the figures in the column labeled "Enlarger," **Column 4.** It is likely that they specify the distance (probably in centimeters) from a negative placed inside the enlarger to the transparent film on which we were trying to capture its image. Toland remembers using numbers on the enlarger's post. My doubt appeared when Holub pointed out that a distance of one centimeter from the table (as we see in Image 6, the horseshoes) would throw the image completely out of focus.

Column 5, "F-Stop," is filled with numbers familiar to anyone who uses a camera that is not completely automatic. An f-stop number indicates a fractional relationship between the focal length of a lens and its aperture. The higher the f-stop number, the smaller the lens opening and the less light can come in.

"Exposure," the heading of **Column 6**, refers to the exposure time, in seconds, used as the enlarger light exposed the image onto the film transparency. Most of the images with f-stops of 16 or higher disappeared. The exceptions, like Image 6, the horseshoes, generally had long exposure times. Holub has checked the images that disappeared, and found that, in their combinations of photographic variables, they simply didn't get enough light. Graphic arts film has more contrast than camera film, he says. You either get the image on there, or you don't.

The next column, **Column 7**, is labeled "Acid," and the numbers in it refer to the amount of time, in minutes, that each image was bitten in acid after it had been put on the plates. An aquatint ground was laid on the plates before biting. The acid bite affected how strongly each image printed. Cage completed this column before he knew which images would disappear (those were not bitten).

Column 8, "Diameter of Image," was filled in by Cage in the darkroom. Whether or not the image was strong enough to be captured on film, it would show in a projection from the negative to the table of the enlarger. Cage measured the projection across its widest part and wrote the measurement in this column. A printer

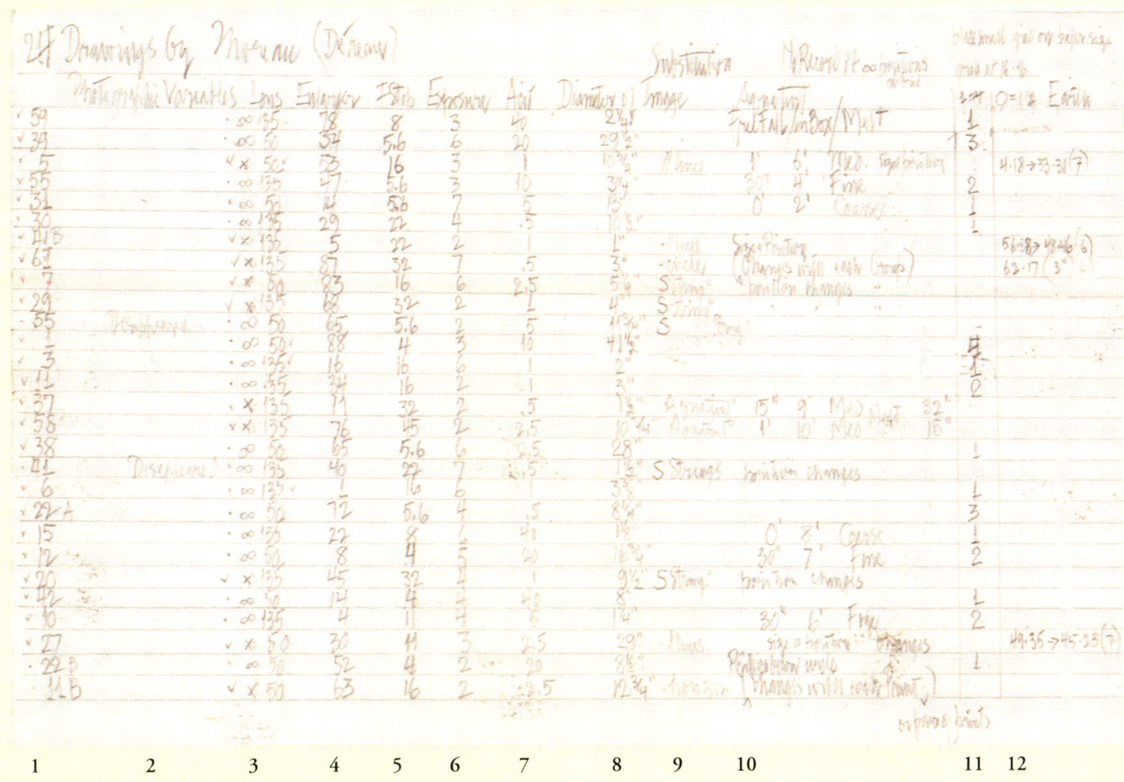

1 2 3 4 5 6 7 8 9 10 11 12

Series score for Déreau.

then cut a piece of film to that length. In the dark, she cut imperfectly, taking from a large roll a piece the approximate size of the image. When the printers were cutting the film pieces, they didn't know that Cage would use some of them as templates for plates to hold replacement images for those not strong enough to appear on the film after it was exposed and developed. It's interesting that the flag-like shape of Image 37, which in a way characterizes *Déreau,* came from a casual gesture rather than from formal chance-derived systems.

Column 9, labeled "Substitution," names the particular images that replaced individuals that disappeared. Cage wrote "|| lines" to indicate bars. The other replacement images were strings, aquatints, a circle, and a horizon.

Column 10 gives information that pertains to the substitution images. For aquatints (used for Images 37 and 58 and in all the Thoreau drawings), Cage has subjected every detail of their creation to chance operations. Aquatints provide areas of tone in etchings. To make them, we use a large plywood box fitted with a fan to dust powdered rosin over the plates. Then we melt the rosin onto the copper. After that, in this case, we bit the aquatints for the times specified in the "Acid" column. Cage has noted in Column 10 how long each plate should be in the aquatint box before and after running the fan, and whether the rosin grains should be fine, medium, or coarse. He has also noted in this column that the sizes of the bars and their positions change with each group of prints, and that the positions of the strings change also.

Cage divided the 38 prints in *Déreau* into ten groups, and the top line of **Columns 11** and **12** refers to the first group of prints, which includes numbers one through four. He made a new circle and a new set of three bars for each group. Here, he specifies that the circle for the first group should have a radius of 1-1/2". Each group has a dominant color palette, and the palette for the first group is Earth.

The numbers in **Column 11**, aside from the first line, refer only to the fixed images. They show whether the image was on plate 1, 2, 3, or 4. Cage filled in this information as he located the images on the plates, adding a new plate whenever necessary. In printing, images in different colors cannot overlap one another unless they are on different plates.

Across the top of the page, over columns 11 and 12, Cage has written: "Place small grid on paper-size grid at 16 · 16." This may refer to locating the floating images in the first group of prints, and/or it may refer to locating the fixed Thoreau images on the large plates. Cage located most of his images on plates in the same way he located plates on the press bed, so it is likely he used a grid, and perhaps two, to locate the fixed images.

In the *On the Surface* project Cage had introduced a small grid (sometimes he called it a floating grid) for use in combination with the paper-sized grid in locating his plates. In *Changes and Disappearances*, images had disappeared if the plates that held them stuck out beyond the paper, but entire plates did not disappear. In *On the Surface* and *Déreau*, because of the small grid, occasionally they did.

To use the small grid, Cage first located it on the paper-sized grid. Frequently, it would hang over the borders. Then, if chance operations directed a plate into the area of the small grid, he would relocate it using the small grid's coordinates. A plate on the small grid could fall out of the picture, and that did happen several times in the *Déreau* series. This is why we are sure Cage used the small grid along with the large one in locating the plates for the floating images in *Déreau*, even though we don't have any notations about it beyond this mention in the score.

The last column of the score, **Column 12**, contains mysterious-looking formulas. I was ready to give up on those, but Lilah Toland figured them out. The short one is for Image 61, the circle, and gives its location in the first print at the spot where vertical gridline 62 crossed horizontal gridline 17. The number in parentheses (3") is the diameter of the circle. Cage used the same circle throughout the first group, but he changed its position in each print.

The other formulas are for the bars. There are two pairs of gridline coordinates because Cage used these formulas for drawing the bars for the first set of prints. To draw the bar that is Image 5, for example, he started at the intersection of vertical gridline 4 and horizontal gridline 18, and drew lines between that point and the point at the intersection of 33 and 31. The number in parentheses (7) shows how many side-by-side lines he drew to create the bar.

He drew a new set of three bars for each group of prints, and changed their locations in each print. To locate each of the three bars in the first print, we think in each formula he used the first pair of coordinates combined with a figure showing the degree to use in turning the plate on a protractor. In the print, we can see that the bars are at angles, so he must have specified information for using the protractor, though we do not see it here.

THE PALETTES. In *Déreau,* Cage used chance operations to divide the 38 prints into ten groups. Each group has a different palette as follows:

1-4, Earth
5, Earth and Red
6-11, Earth and Blue
12-14, Yellow
15, Blue
16, Yellow
17-22, Earth and Blue
23-30, Yellow
31, Black and Yellow
32-38, Earth and Blue.

Cage took the 45 ink colors we had available at Crown Point Press at the time, and divided them into five palettes: Black, Yellow, Red, Blue, and Earth. In this case, he didn't use chance operations but placed each ink color into the category into which he and the printers agreed it belonged. Then, for each print he used chance operations to determine the dominant palette, a possible secondary palette, and the particular colors within them. Then he asked whether to add a color outside the chosen palettes, and if the answer was yes, he chose one of the 45 original colors. Finally, he asked his chance operations whether there should be white added and, if so, in what proportion.

On the page facing this one, you can see the individual score for Print 7, along with its map and a small reproduction of the print itself, which we have reversed to make the map easy to read. Print 7 is part of the third group, with palettes of Earth and Blue. If we read down the score we can see that the first image on the list, 59, is cerulean blue. Since it has no coordinates listed for locating it, we know it is a fixed image, and a glance at the Key to the Fixed Images on page 72 shows us that it is a bug-like shape. Image 39, a swirl, is printed in a mixture that is 80 percent cerulean and 20 percent burnt sienna with 2/5 white. Image 5 is floating—it has location numbers. It is printed in raw umber, and we can see by the map that it is one of the bars. Cage located it at the juncture of grid coordinates vertical 49 and horizontal 55, and then turned it against a protractor to 68 degrees (it fell partly outside the sheet). If you try to reconstruct the locations of the images using the coordinates listed, most of them (like this one) appear where you would expect. But remember that we are not sure where the small grid was in each case, and its possible use is a wild card.

Continuing to read down the score, I could find two colors outside the Earth and Blue palettes: cadmium yellow light is mixed with cobalt in Image 61, the circle, and strontium yellow is mixed with raw sienna in Image 58, the larger and lighter of the two aquatints.

Notice that only the strings and the aquatints have

7

59 Cerulean
39 Cerulean Brt. S. 8020 + 3/5 W
5 Raw U 49.55 68°
55B Mars Y + 1/5 W
31 Milori Y O M 8020
30 Mars Mo Red 8020
41B UM 43.44 319°
61 Cobalt CYL 7030 + 3/7 W 18.52
7 Cerulean + 48.44 CD 140°
29 UM Lilac B 5050 31.13 BC 149°
55A Raw S + 1/10 W 35.51 BC 337°
1 Mars V Indigo 1090
3 Raw S
11 Milori + 3/5 W
37 YOL Mars V 8020 9.3 BC 74°
58 Raw S Str. Y 2080 2.60 AB 318°
38 Mars B
41 Mars B + 46.39 AB 64°
6 Mang.
22A UM + 1/2 W
15 Milori
12 Mang. + 1/2 W
20 Cobalt + 1/10 W 18.62 AB 18°
42 Milori + 1/4 W
10 Permanent + 1/2 W
27 Raw Sienna 32.50 273°
22B Van Dyke + 2/3 W
11B Mars 39

Individual Score for Déreau 7. *This print is part of a large group that contains Prints 7 through 22.*

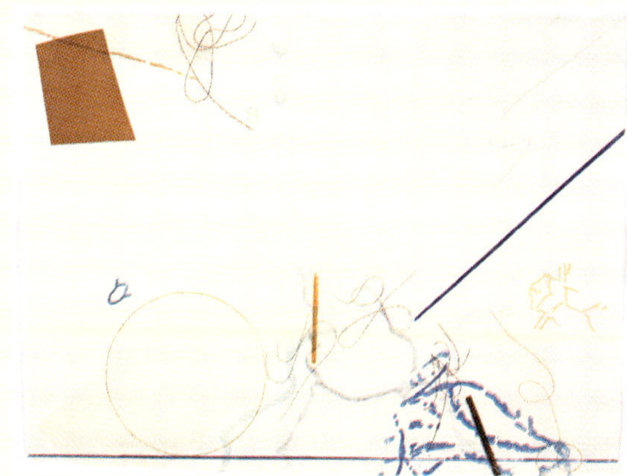

Déreau 7 *(reversed). The print in its correct orientation is shown on page 20.*

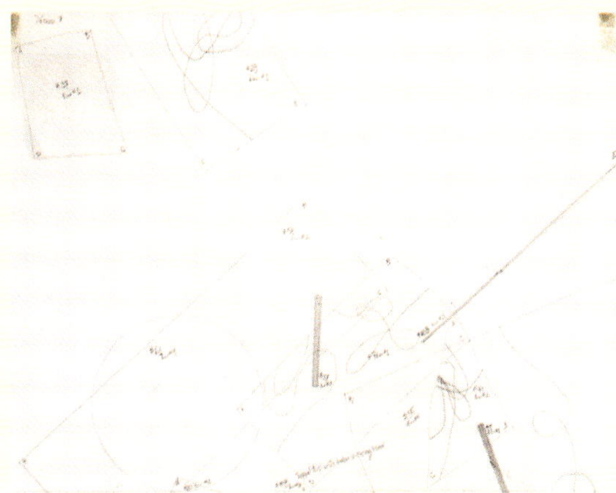

Map for the Floating Images, Déreau 7.

letters to indicate the plate edges used for orienting them against the protractor. The lines, unlike the strings and aquatints, have clear horizontals that could be placed on the selected horizontal gridlines, then turned as the protractor directed. The circle (61) does not have degrees specified, since it is not turned. And the horizon (11B) has only one number, that of the horizontal gridline on which it falls. But wait! The number after the horizon is crossed out. What does that mean?

If you turn back to the score, you might be able to make out a note on the second line from the bottom in Column 10. It refers to the horizon, and it says, "position below circle." The circle (61) is at horizontal gridline 52, very low on the sheet. It is much lower than the horizon (11B) would have been if it had been located at gridline 39. Cage has written "Tangent to circle, with paper showing below," on the map at Image 11B, the horizon. If the circle had been even lower, (sometimes it falls partly off the page), the horizon would be as low as possible, with no paper showing.

At last we are at the end of this Section of Detail, this Book Within a Book. I hope I have not disillusioned someone who loves John Cage because he was so "free"! He *was*, in fact, free—free of petty judgments and discontents, free to see unexpected things, and certainly free to learn. If you made it through this section you learned something about discipline and devotion, as I did in writing it. In all time-honored traditions of spirituality, practitioners are asked not to add meaning to the practice, but instead to follow the letter of it.

Retallack remarked that in Cage's work "mistakes" can change to "possibilities" and Cage replied in this way: "I think the nature of the difference between graphic work and the musical work brought about a change of feelings. At least gave me new experiences. I'm trying to say that I was made happy by *not* slipping, and not only happy, but as though I had done something, accomplished something."[27]

That Cage thought about the nature of this "change of feelings" at the time is shown in a videotape I made in 1979. Cage was deeply involved in plates with even more engraved lines, and more difficult ones, than there are in *Signals.* "It seemed to me that to be able to engrave required a certain calmness," he says on the tape. "And it's that calmness that I've been, one way or another, approaching in my music and writing and so forth. And then, it became physical, you see, with the engraving tool."[28]

It seems to me that in 1978, the first year of Cage's work at Crown Point in visual art, he arrived at the most serious and irrevocable aspect of his work: *devotion.*

The Big Sets of Prints, 1979-1982. Devotion was required, both on Cage's part and that of his printers, for the *Changes and Disappearances* project that came next. Cage was writing the Freeman Etudes at the time. In this work, he said, "I wanted to make the music as difficult as possible so that a performance would show that the impossible is not impossible."[29] The *Changes and Disappearances* prints, he remarked in another context, "were as complicated as things could be. As complicated as, say, the Freeman Etudes. It was difficult for the printers to realize the work. I like them very much. They're probably the most musical, the most detailed work with very subtle changes in the colors and shapes. ...Just as music is made with lots of little notes, so this is made with all those little pieces of color."[30]

Changes and Disappearances is printed on rectangular sheets of pale gray-blue paper. The prints have what look like translucent panes of glass drifting across them, the light catching on slender images imbedded in the panes. The images are on sixty-six small plates, each with a curvy side, the curves made by cutting with a jig saw over strings Cage had dropped on the plate. (He mentioned that he was imitating Duchamp, who had dropped strings to obtain curves in a work of sculpture, *Three Standard Stoppages*, in 1913.)

There are many curving lines, since Cage also dropped strings to get marks over which he engraved, and many straight ones that he scratched into the plates using drypoint.

Cage added the engraving and drypoint lines one by one as he added new prints to the series. Sometimes after lines were drawn and colors specified, when the plates were set out on the press bed, a line would fall outside the paper borders. Cage called this a disappearance.

"Do I have to mix the colors for a line even if it disappears?" asks printer Lilah Toland on grainy black and white videotape that I shot in the studio more than twenty years ago. It is dark outside, and raining. Cage, Toland, and her assistant are in a pool of light by a worktable leaning over Cage's piles of papers covered with charts and numbers.

"No, sweetie," Cage replies. "I'm not going to give you any unnecessary work." It is the end of the day and they open bottles of beer. Toland is counting, a chart in front of her. "Forty-five!" she exclaims. "Forty-five colors, and that's just for the first print. I think I'll end up in Napa State Hospital. I'll be sitting there saying, 'BC to CD is four parts manganese blue to two parts titanium white.'" They are laughing now.

"Oh, it's going to be horrendous!" Cage says, passing a hand over his eyes.

"Each print will have more colors," Toland says. "I'll bet we could easily get up to 200 colors! I think it's time to program some emptiness into this project."

They are all laughing hard, Cage so much that he can hardly speak. "Zukofsky [the violinist for whom he was writing

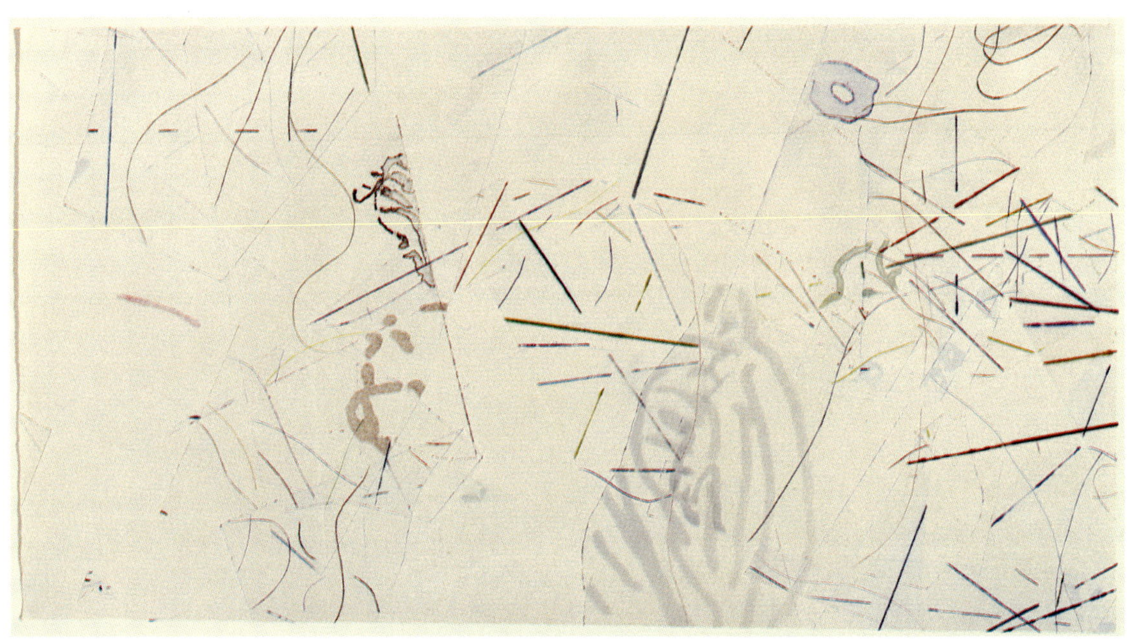

Changes and Disappearances 31, 1979-1982. *One in a series of 35 engravings with drypoint and photoetching, printed by Lilah Toland at Crown Point Press in two or three impressions each. 11 x 22" (28 x 56 cm).*

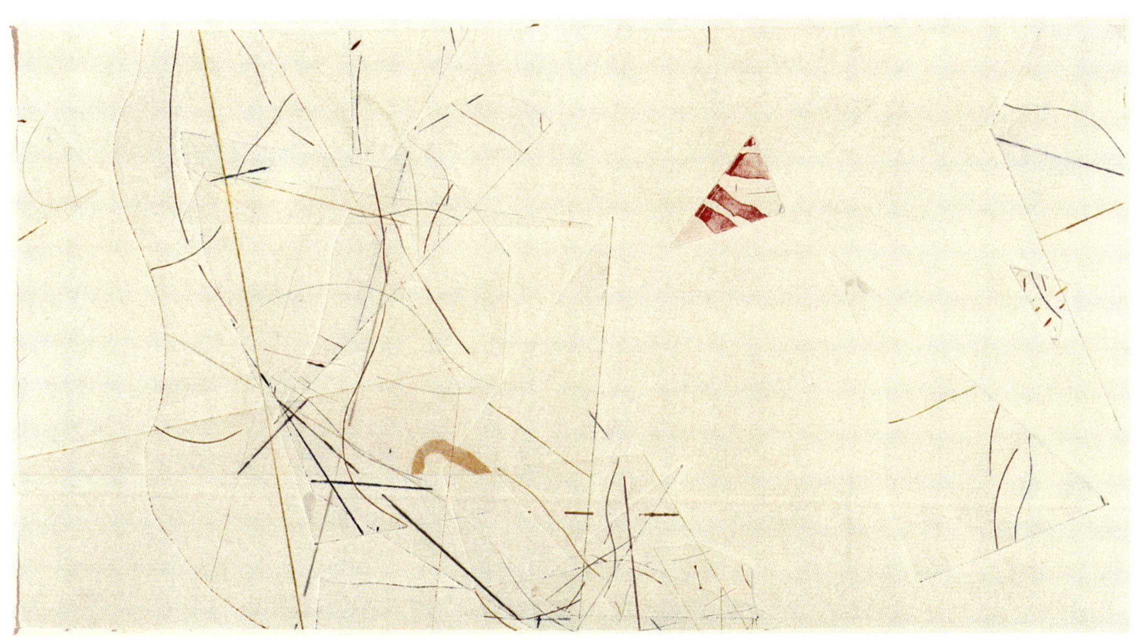

Changes and Disappearances 16. *One of two impressions.*

the Freeman Etudes] said to me, 'You must find some way of writing music that isn't so difficult.' I said, 'What do you mean?' He said, 'Well, look at my wrists. I cannot continue!'"

The first *Changes and Disappearances* print ended up with 54 colors. The last one, Number 35, done four years later, has 298. We printed two impressions of each of these prints (with a third in a few cases for artist's proofs).

By Cage's fifth work period on *Changes and Disappearances*, in September 1980, we had begun training two new printers, and Cage had an idea for a set of prints that he proposed could be done by them at the same time as the project in progress. He wanted to use the beautiful hand tone he had discovered in working on *Signals*, and he wanted to add the concept of a horizon line. The new project, *On the Surface,* was inspired by Cage's memory of clams rising to the surface in an aquarium—Cage describes that memory in the quotation that opens this chapter.

The prints are on very white handmade paper. The small individual plates appear as shards floating, overlapping, nudging one another against an implied horizon line that lowers in each print in the series. At a glance the paper seems blank except for the shadows of the embossed edges of the plates, but pale colors soon come into focus, along with many fine dashes, peppered dots, and other lovely accidental marks.

Sixty-four plates taken from our scrap pile were individually shaped, each with one curved side, and located according to chance operations. As the series progressed, whenever a plate poked up over the horizon it was cut again from a point on the horizon line to a chance-determined point below. There was an exception, however. If a plate settled into a position where the portion below the line was too small to cut cleanly, it remained uncut and was lightly balanced above the others.

We began the *On the Surface* project in 1980 and finished in 1982, with two impressions printed of each image.

Déreau, the last of the big sets and to me in some ways the most satisfying, was entirely done in 1982, the year we also finished both *Changes and Disappearances* and *On the Surface.* As I think back on *Déreau*, it is as if it somehow just grew up naturally as work on the other two enormous projects was coming to a close.

Cage made up the word "Déreau" using the first syllable of "décor" and the second of "Thoreau." The entire set is illustrated earlier in this book. Fixed Thoreau drawings provide a décor, or stage-set, for free-floating elements. Although Cage's composition (evidenced by the score) was more complex than for the previous two big sets, the printers' work was less arduous. The prints are more visually expansive than those in the earlier sets.

We see some animal and bird tracks, part of a flower, something that might be a waterbug. There are bubbles near the top of the page, and a swirl of waving lines in several colors at the bottom. A circle dances onto this stage, and some bars. The most active figures are the intricate engravings; they are taut with energy. There is a horizon line, but it doesn't relate to the forms. It moves up and down in the different prints in the series, changing everything by implying the sea below, the sky above.

The colors in *Déreau* are from five distinct palettes: black, yellow, red, blue, and earth. Cage once told me he wanted his colors "to look like they went to graduate school," and they were always complex mixtures in chance-determined proportions. This is the only series, however, that sets out several distinct palettes; there are subtle but unmistakable passages of color change.

Changes and Disappearances (35 prints), *On the Surface* (36 prints), and *Déreau* (38 prints) are major works of Cage's visual art. He saw these sets as large complex single works, the parts of which, to his great delight, could be dispersed independently without disturbing the whole. For each of these works, at his request, we printed a "posterity" set that is kept

On the Surface 5, *1980-1982. One in a series of 35 related images in two impressions each. Printed by Paul Singdahlsen at Crown Point Press. 18-1/2 x 24-1/2" (47 x 62 cm).*

On the Surface 29. *In each successive print, the horizon lowers. Plates that protruded over the horizon were cut unless the part below or above the line was so small as to make cutting impractical. If a plate was cut, the parts created a "family," and sometimes (because of successive cuts) families grew to four or more members, with a, b, c, and d added to the original plate number. Anytime the plate number was selected for inclusion in a print, the entire family would appear.*

together, and also one or two individual prints of each image.

In Cage's list of aspects of his work, it is the word *discipline* that most applies to the 1979-1982 period of his art making. On that list, he said he had originally included "form" but it was absorbed into "discipline." "The form—in other words, what happens—comes about through chance, and is, so to speak, not connected as a concern."[31] What happened in these large works, I believe, is a new form, not seen in art before. This form is something akin to birds flying or fish swimming. It is released from the picture plane, and doesn't pull people into it dramatically. When you first notice it, you wonder if it's really there.

After these works, Cage changed practically everything in his approach. He had learned to engrave with a skill few printmakers accomplish, but these are the last works in which he used engraving. They are also the last ones in which Thoreau drawings came into play. Finally, they are the last works he characterized as detailed in a way that he thought of as musical.

III. SIMPLIFYING WITH STONES AND FIRE

> Now and then I come across an article on that rock garden in Japan where there's just a space of sand and a few rocks in it. The author, no matter who he is, sets out either to suggest that the position of the rocks in the space follows some geometrical plan productive of the beauty one observes, or not satisfied with mere suggestion, he makes diagrams and detailed analyses. So when I met Ashihara, the Japanese music and dance critic (his first name escapes me), I told him that I thought those stones could have been anywhere in that space, that I doubted whether their relationship was a planned one, that the emptiness of the sand was such that it could support stones at any points in it. Ashihara had already given me a present (some table mats), but then he asked me to wait a moment while he went into his hotel. He came out and gave me the tie I am now wearing.
>
> —John Cage in *A Year from Monday,* 1963[32]

Horizontal and Vertical: Crown Point Press, 1983-1987. The Drawings, New York City, 1983-1992. The Watercolors: Mountain Lake, Virginia, 1988 and 1990. When Cage arrived at Crown Point Press on January 2, 1983, he brought with him a bag of stones, sixteen of them, each two to three inches across. As he pulled them out of his suitcase, he reported gleefully that the baggage porter had asked, "What have you got in here, rocks?" He also brought an idea to buy some soft packing materials—cotton batting, jute pads, felt, and foam—and use those to make prints. That idea was realized as *HV.*

HV stands for Horizontal/Vertical, and these strange one-of-a-kind prints, in which irregular, unruly materials were asked to function geometrically, set the tone for all the work to come. Cage's intention in his January 1983 work period at

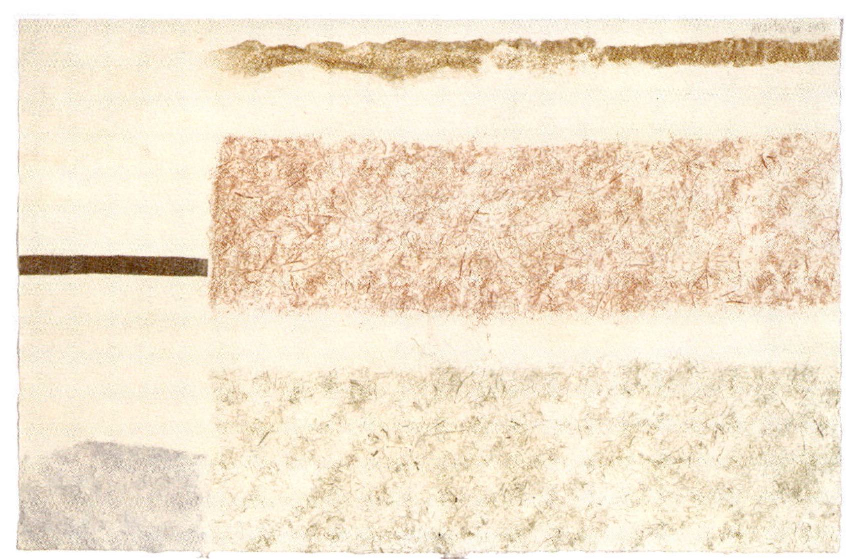

HV, 1983. *Number 2 in a series of 36 monotype collagraphs, each one unique. Printed by Lilah Toland at Crown Point Press. Sheet size 11-3/4 x 18-1/2" (30 x 47 cm).*

HV, *Number 11, unique.*

Crown Point, I believe, was to make something with a horizontal/vertical orientation that was also bumpy. The new work—as he had written years before about the music of David Tudor—would "keep the ineptitudes, to reveal not something perfect but something that showed that he had been alive while making it."[33]

Cage used the stones he had brought with him to begin what turned out to be a large and absorbing body of work that he titled collectively *Ryoanji.* The *Ryoanji* prints have dimensions proportionate to those of the Ryoanji Garden in Kyoto, Japan. From the sixteen stones he had brought, Cage selected fifteen, the number in the famous garden. He located each stone individually on a single test plate using his system of coordinates on a grid, but keeping a horizontal/vertical axis that did not require use of the protractor that had figured so prominently in the earlier work. He drew around the stones with a sharp drypoint tool. The first test failed. He wasn't satisfied with the way it looked, so he moved to more complex

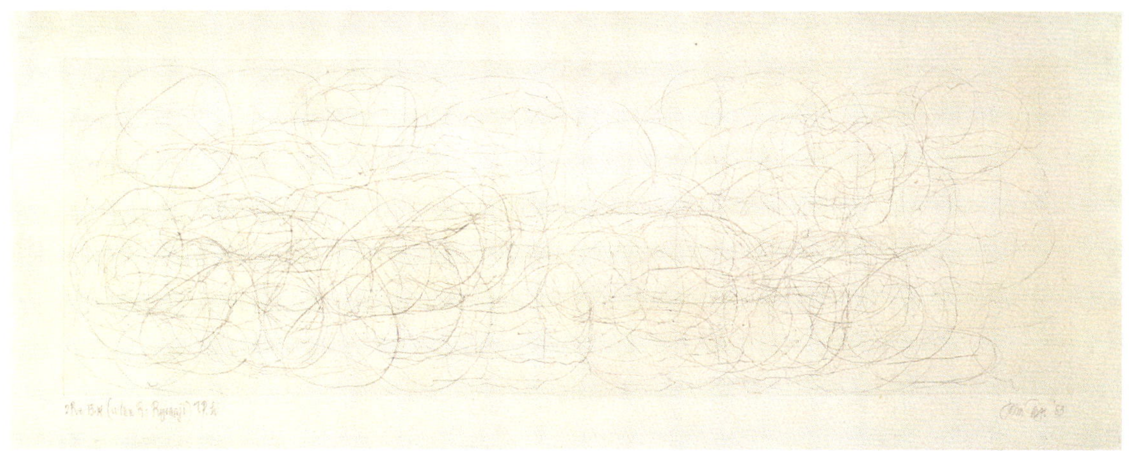

Where R=Ryoanji: 2R+13·14, 1983. *Drypoint. Printed in an edition of 25 by Lilah Toland at Crown Point Press. 7 x 21" (18 x 54 cm) on 9 x 24" sheet (23 x 61 cm).*

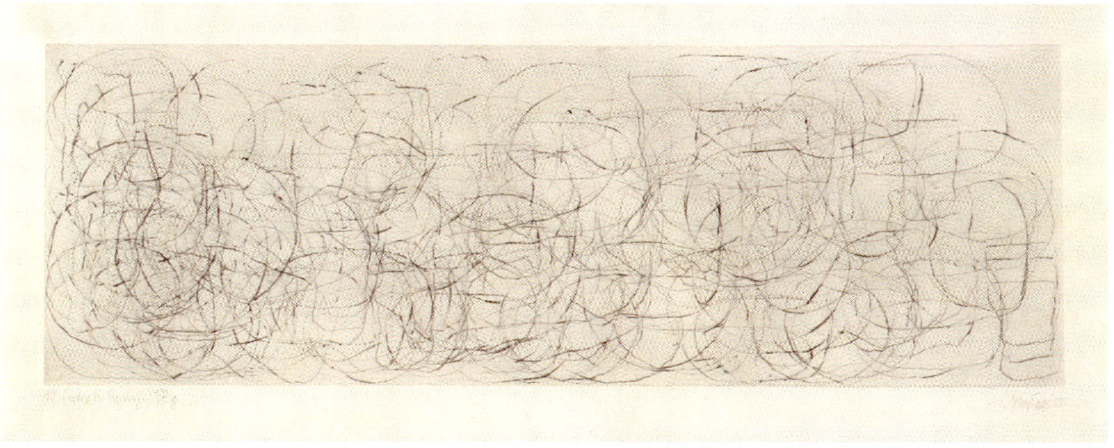

Where R=Ryoanji: $R^2$1, 1983. *Drypoint, edition 25.*

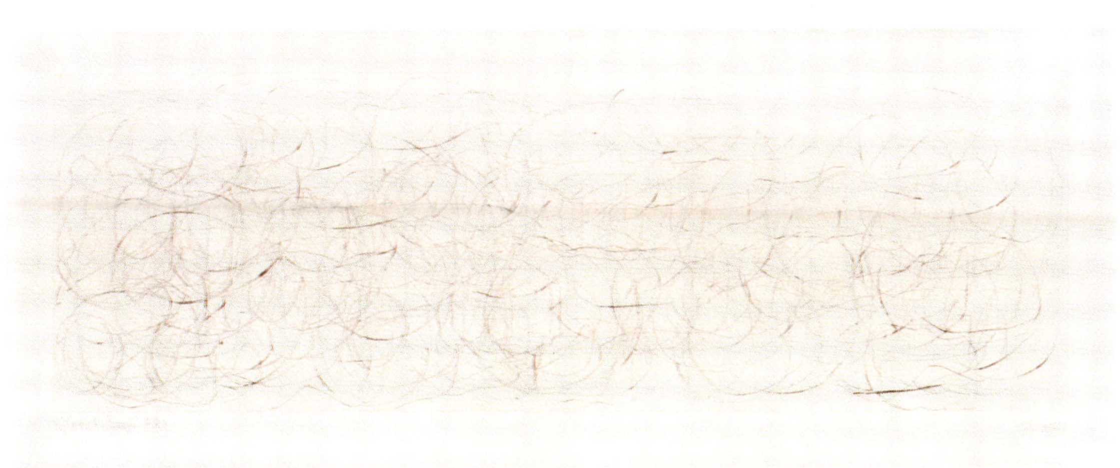

Where R=Ryoanji R²2, 1983. *Drypoint, edition 25.*

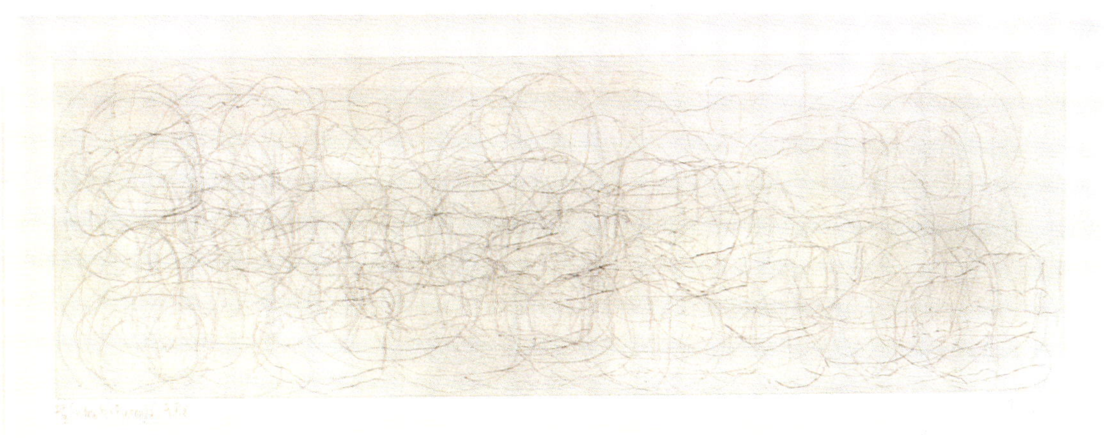

Where R=Ryoanji R²3, 1983. *Drypoint, edition 25.*

Where R=Ryoanji: R^3, 1983. *Drypoint, edition 25.*

questions. Later, I learned that Cage had made a *Ryoanji* drawing of fifteen stones on paper in 1982 as a cover design for one of a series of books called *Editions Ryoan-ji.* When he tried the same thing on metal, he wrote, "The mystery produced by pencils disappeared, reappearing only on copper when the number of stones was multiplied."[34]

The prints, as a group, are titled *Where R=Ryoanji,* and each has an individual subtitle that describes the system used to make it. Once you realize that R=15 stones, it's easy to understand the subtitles of both the prints and the drawings, which (except for the book cover) came later and are titled similarly. In the first print, *2R+13·14,* Cage drew around two stones fifteen times each, then drew around thirteen stones fourteen times each. The result was good, but after that he changed his approach. He had received the numbers 13 and 14 from his chance operations, but as he went on he turned to multiplying the number of stones in a more direct way.

He worked with R squared, which entailed 225 drawings on a plate. He repeated that approach three times, using different amounts of pressure on his tool—*$R^2 1$* is drawn with light pressure, *$R^2 2$* with medium pressure, and in *$R^2 3$* he pressed heavily. Since drypoint lines are simply scratched into the copper plate, the tool throws up a burr that collects ink against it. As Cage's tool traveled around each rock, it threw

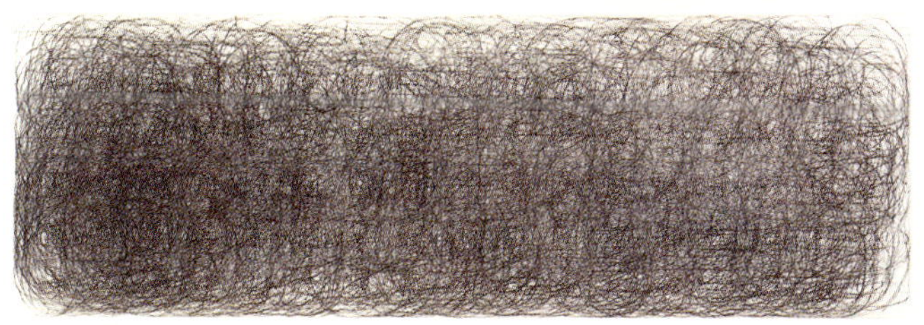

Where R=Ryoanji: (R^3), 1983. *Drypoint, edition 25.*

up a thicker burr wherever he tipped it at an angle, so the lines are irregular and lively.

He was just getting started on *R^3*, which entailed 3,375 drawings around individually placed rocks, when it was time to leave. So he packed up his tool, the plate, and another plate and went back to New York.

In the four earlier prints, he had turned the stones so they would fall entirely within the boundaries of the plate. In *R^3* he didn't do this, and because there are so many stone drawings the plate becomes a mesh of lines, something like steel wool. In *(R^3)*, a second print containing the same number of drawings, he went back to turning the stones inward. In his subsequent work with stones and rocks, he generally kept them fully inside the paper.

"You can cut a piece of copper," Cage told Retallack, "but if you're working as I do when I make drawings—if you're working with stones—you can't cut the stone, hmm? It's not practical. So the stone is either in the drawing or not. And I choose that it is! (laughs) ... [Otherwise], it gives a feeling that doesn't seem, so to speak, at home with me. ...I don't feel as though I've *honored*, say the rock or the Thoreau image."[35]

Perhaps it was a spirit of honoring the stones, perhaps an attempt to simplify, possibly an impulse toward "nonobstruction" of the horizontal that led Cage with this series to aban-

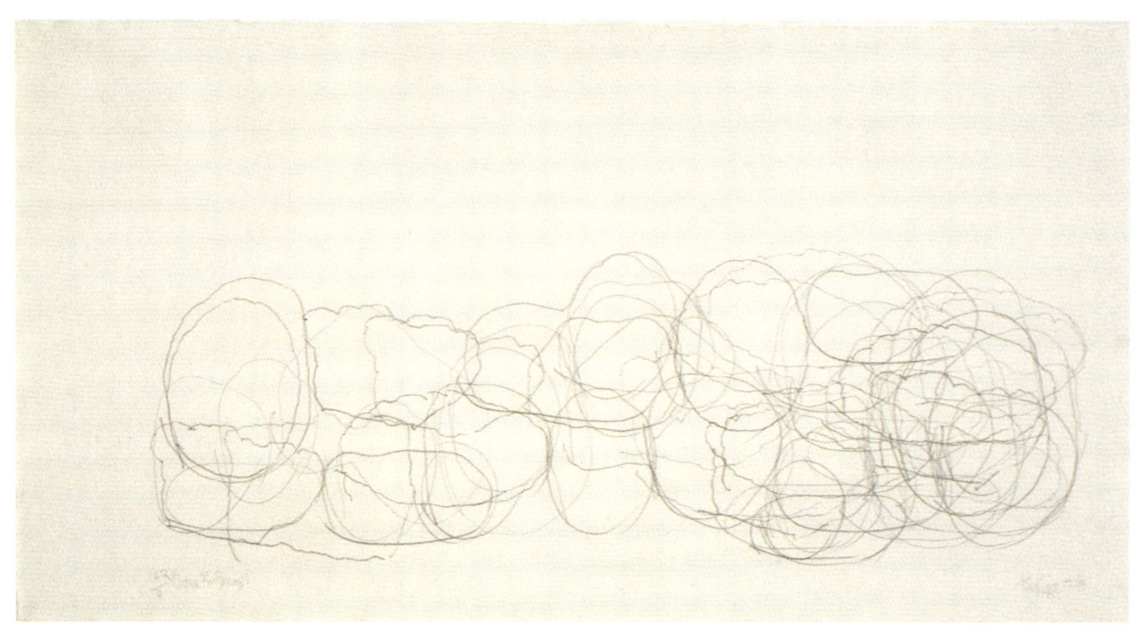

Where R=Ryoanji (4R)4 7-83, 1983. *Pencil on paper. 10 x 19" (25 x 48 cm).*

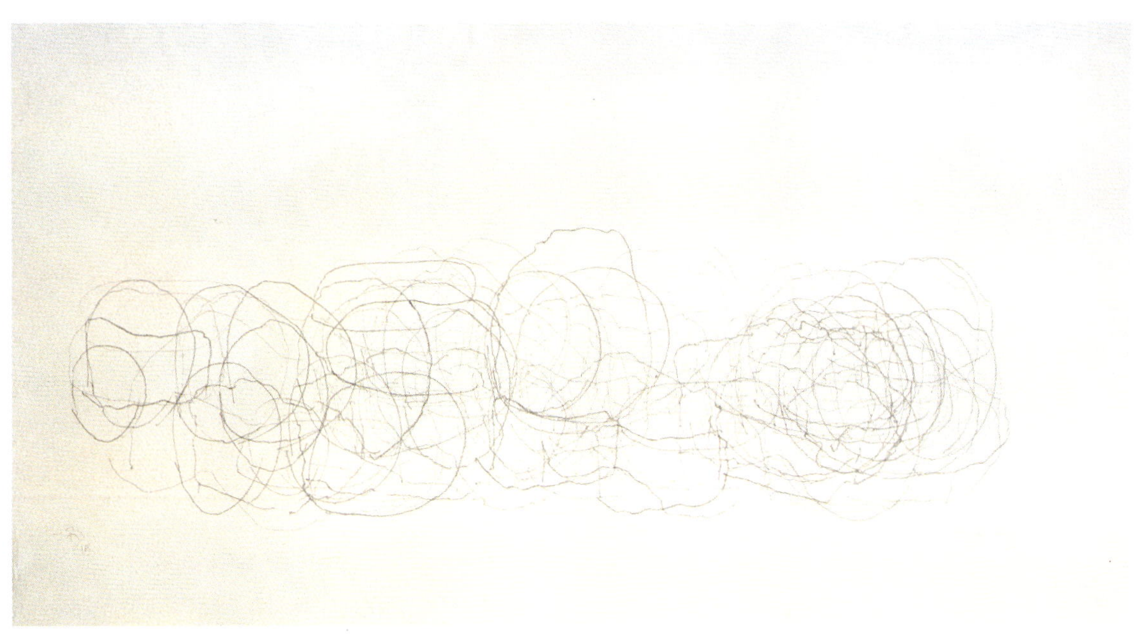

Where R=Ryoanji R8/15, 1992. *Pencil on paper. 10 x 19" (25 x 48 cm).*

don using a protractor to locate his images. Certainly many Thoreau images were fragmented in the earlier prints, and the stones could have been treated the same way without physically cutting them. In all the *Ryoanji* work, however, Cage simply placed the stones "right-side up" at the *I Ching* selected coordinates of his paper-sized grid, and turned them only as necessary.

Cage began drawing on paper after he finished work on the two plates he had with him in New York. Margarete Roeder, his friend and longtime art dealer, says that he used his drawing activity as a kind of meditation. He often spoke of writing music "instead of sitting cross-legged," and by the time he began drawing in 1983 some of the labor-intensive part of writing music had been taken over by the computer.

So far as making an actual drawing was concerned, he must have enjoyed the ease with which his pencils moved around the rocks after having done so much scratching into copper with a sharp point. The drawings are not as bumpy as the prints. Cage drew them with pencils of varying hardness, from 6B to 9H, and the number of pencils used is shown as the last number in the title. As in the prints, R equals 15. So R8/15 would mean there are fifteen times eight stone tracings done with fifteen different pencils. He never used any other approach for his drawings—they are all *Ryoanji.*

There is *Ryoanji* music too; it provides flights of glissandi for the instruments involved. Probably the prints came first (they were begun in January 1983 and the music called *Ryoanji* is dated 1983-1984), but, in any case, Cage points out to Retallack that the two are composed differently. "There [in the graphic work] I'm not dealing with time, so I can draw around the whole stone. Music is characterized by detail and by having to do things that work in time." He added that in drawing around the stones for music he created curved lines that go "from left to right as music does. They don't go in a circle. Music doesn't go in a circle. The only way a circle could be expressed in music would be with two instruments, both of which went from left to right [one ascending, the other descending]."[36]

Except for his drawing, music occupied Cage fully in 1984. In January 1985 he returned to Crown Point for a two-week period, bringing his stones. We used them for *Ryoku,* a set of thirteen lovely color drypoints that seemed—like *Déreau*—almost to occur of their own accord. *Ku* in the title stands for an association with Haiku. There are seventeen syllables in a Haiku poem, and in *Ryoku* Cage used seventeen earth and mineral pigments, combined in equal parts through chance operations to get ten colors. Only cobalt green combined with itself, and since it is the only pure pigment the prints have a delicate feeling of being green. Cage used the same stones for all the *Ryoanji* and *Ryoku* work, and perhaps it was his familiarity with them that allowed each one, in his mind, to have a top and bottom. In *Ryoku,* he traced the stones on individual shards of copper, and in locating the copper pieces in the prints he kept the stones upright. In the printing, there is hand tone along with his tremulous lines, so the stones seem gently encased in pale shapes. They group themselves across sheets of handmade paper and are quietly radiant.

At the same time, Cage was looking for a direction that didn't include the stones. He thought it might be promising to try some experiments with earth, air, fire, and water. He cut up different papers and subjected them to the elements by burying them, burning them, soaking them in dirty water and tea, and driving over them with a car (he had done this long ago in helping Rauschenberg with a print of his). He also ran some through the press with damp teabags and branded some with heated iron teapots (he said he had brands like that on the kitchen counter at home). We ended up with nine unique collages somewhat Rauschenbergian in feel, and two good ideas: using fire and using brands.

Right then, before he left, Cage made 16 works called *Fire,* on tall pieces of paper that were subjected to fires we built on the bed of the press. The paper was damp, and running it

Ryoku 6, *edition 10. One in a series of thirteen drypoints printed in an edition of 10 by Marcia Bartholme at Crown Point Press. Sheet size 18 x 24" (46 x 61 cm).*

Ryoku 8, *edition 10.*

through the press put out the fire and trapped the swirling smoke marks, to which Cage added branding. Chance operations dictated which teapots from a group we had assembled made the brand marks and how many to use in each print. Cage loved the way these smoked paper surfaces looked, and he used fire as a medium for the next seven years until he died.

The following year, 1986, we spent the first day of Cage's work period in a junkyard pulling on massive pieces of twisted iron. Eventually we managed to separate one link from a chain that had been on a hoist, and that gave us a branding tool in the form of a large circle, an *en* in Japanese. *Enso* paintings, which Cage had in mind, are circles drawn by monks. *Ka* means "fire" in Japanese. The prints we did in 1986 are called *Eninka.*

At first, I wondered if we would get any prints. We made many tests, counting newspaper balls as instructed by chance operations and timing burns and brands, but despite the beautiful circle we couldn't seem to do anything that advanced the *Fire* prints from the previous year.

Cage thought we should try lots of different kinds of paper and even though it seemed impractical we tested a sheet of *gampi*, a skin-like Japanese paper so thin it can only be used for printing if it is mounted to something heavier. The big fire selected at first by chance demolished it, but Cage adjusted the parameters that controlled fire size and soon we were able to pull some large pieces out of the pile of ashes on the press. Cage was fascinated that the paper was so sensitive that it picked up occasional imprints from the newspapers used for the fire. Still, he was dejected. "It's just a mess," he said.

"Wait," said Marcia Bartholme, his chief printer at the time. She tossed the crumpled and burned papers into a bath of water. Soon they straightened out, and after mounting ("It's what we would normally do with this paper," Bartholme explained) suddenly we had a map-like form, or a seaside landscape. Cage was suffused with joy.

"Oh, it's beautiful! Don't you think it's beautiful? I can't

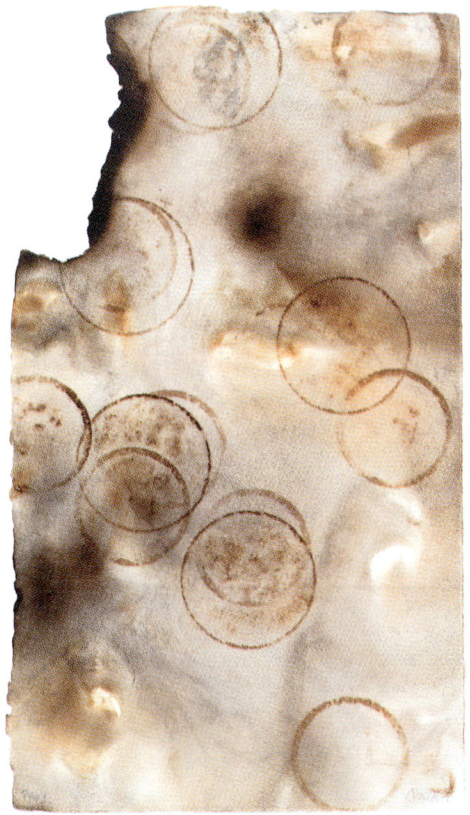

Fire 1, 1985. *One in a series of sixteen unique smoked and branded prints. Printed by Peter Pettengill at Crown Point Press. Approximate sheet size 12 x 20" (30 x 51 cm).*

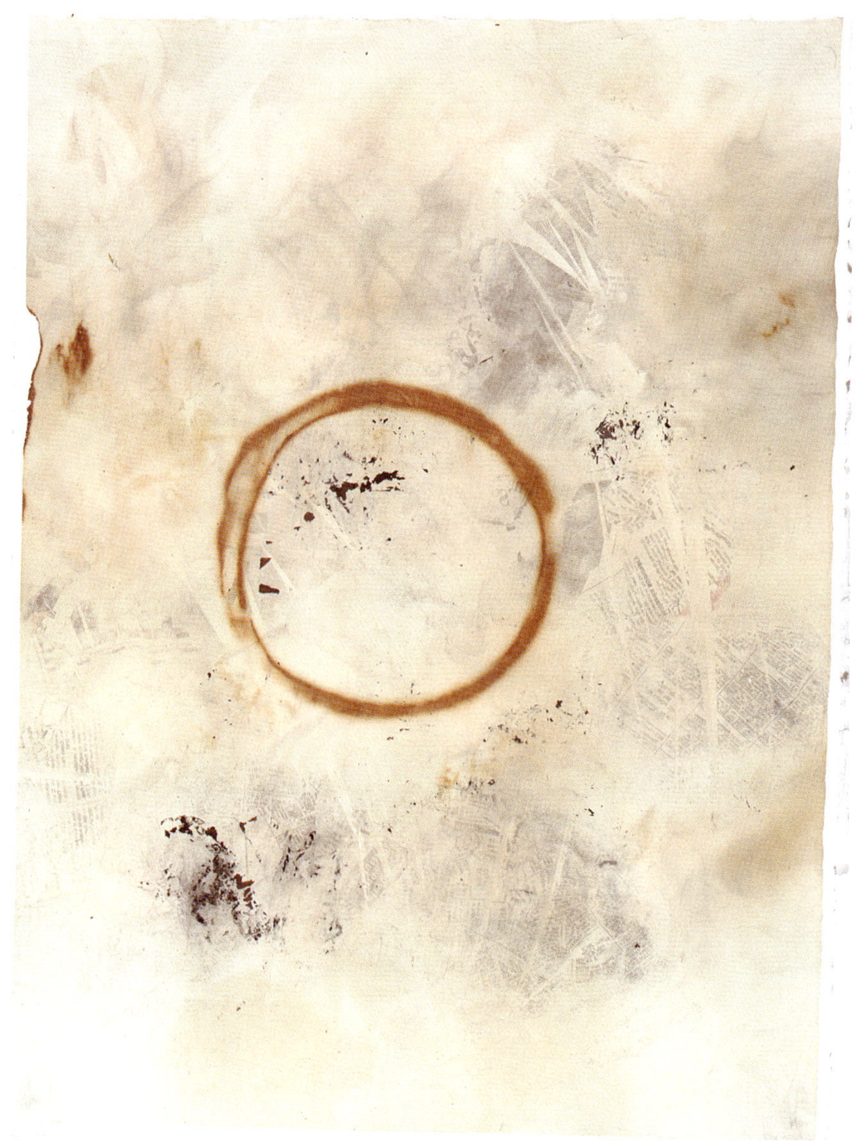

Eninka 17, 1986. *One in a series of fifty unique smoked and branded prints on* gampi *paper* chine collé. *Printed by Marcia Bartholme at Crown Point Press. 25 x 19" (64 x 48 cm).*

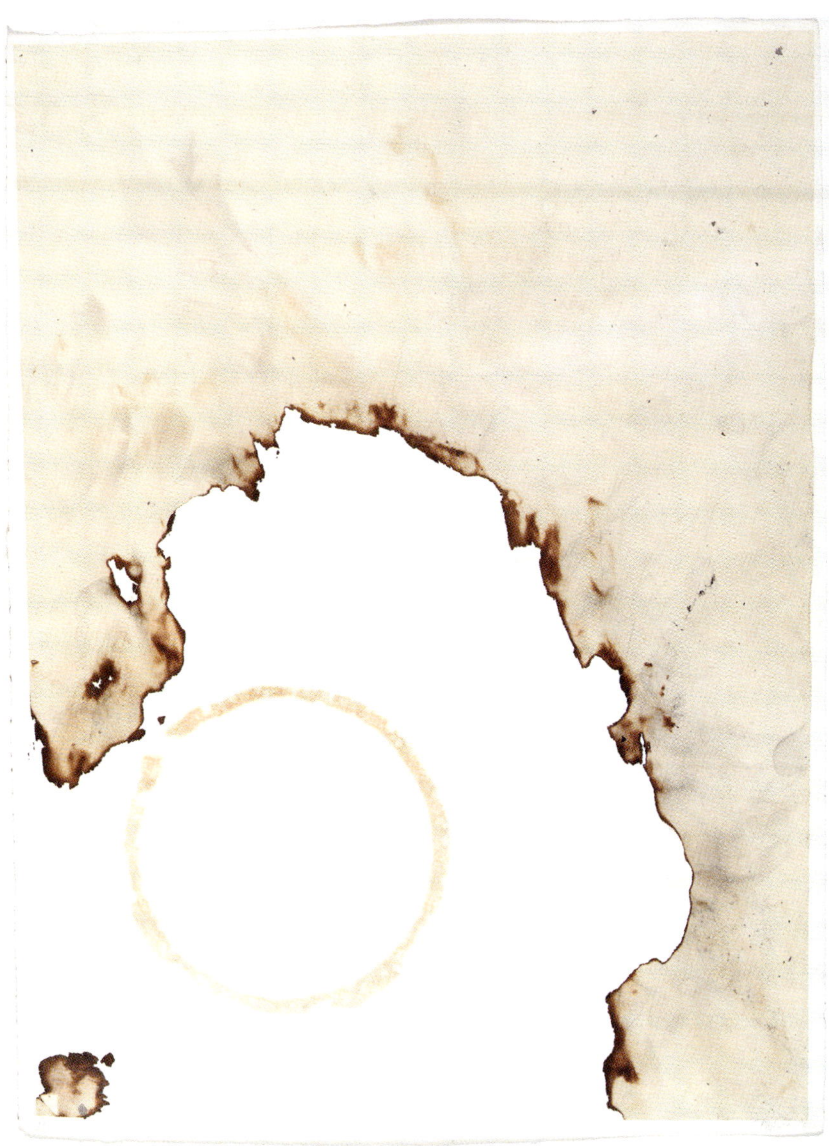

Eninka 42, *unique.*

believe it. I couldn't sleep all night. I thought my whole life had been a waste!"[37] He was laughing, of course, but it made me think. Once he got started on a path, he might make adjustments but he wouldn't set out in a different direction until the path arrived somewhere. Each time something seemed to be a mess did he wonder, if only briefly, if his whole life had been a waste?

In this group of prints Cage concentrated on *structure*. I think his underlying question was how soft or hard the structure needed to be. In the following year, 1987, when he did a series called *Déka*, it became clear that structure was somehow in his mind. As in *Déreau*, the first part of the title stands for "décor." The second part, *ka*, is the Japanese work for "fire." Before and after 1987, Cage used fire by smoking the printing

Déka, 1987. *Aquatint with flat bite etching, one in a series of 45 unique prints. 16 x 19" (41 x 49 cm).*

paper. Here, he etched into a plate the residue of soot and smoke from a fire. Then he combined that plate with another that contained a "stage," a chance-decided geometric shape running along the bottom of the sheet.

The Watercolors, Mountain Lake Workshop, Virginia, 1988 and 1990. In 1983, the year Cage did the first prints and drawings using stones, he was invited to Virginia to lecture at an exhibition of his etchings at the Virginia Polytechnic Institute and State University. At the last minute, Cage had asked that some of his new drawings be included. Ray Kass, an instructor at the Institute with a specialty in watercolor, was very taken with them, and invited Cage to do some similar work in watercolor.

During Cage's 1983 visit to Virginia, Kass did two things to lay the groundwork for the future watercolors. He took Cage to the nearby New River and showed him the large round rocks there, and he prepared what he called a "studio practice" with rocks, papers, brushes, and watercolors in place. He hoped Cage would locate the rocks using his chance operations and then draw around them using the watercolors, and also he "suggested [Cage] apply some surface washes in order to experience the transparency of the medium and its layering effect."[38] Cage did some tests. Five years later he did a full-fledged workshop. He spent eight days in 1988 working with Kass and a few students. He drew around the rocks, which were so beautifully round that most of the tracings can be seen as circles, and he added washes using large flat brushes, several of which Kass designed and had constructed especially for him. He made fifty-two works, which he collectively titled *New River Watercolors.*

Kass has written a detailed account of that workshop and in it he says Cage at first was "not sure what he was doing here," and at the beginning the watercolors were "too heavy and concrete."[39] The color was too wet and pooled uncontrollably and there were too many mixtures, too many rocks. Cage kept making adjustments, and eventually reached a group in which

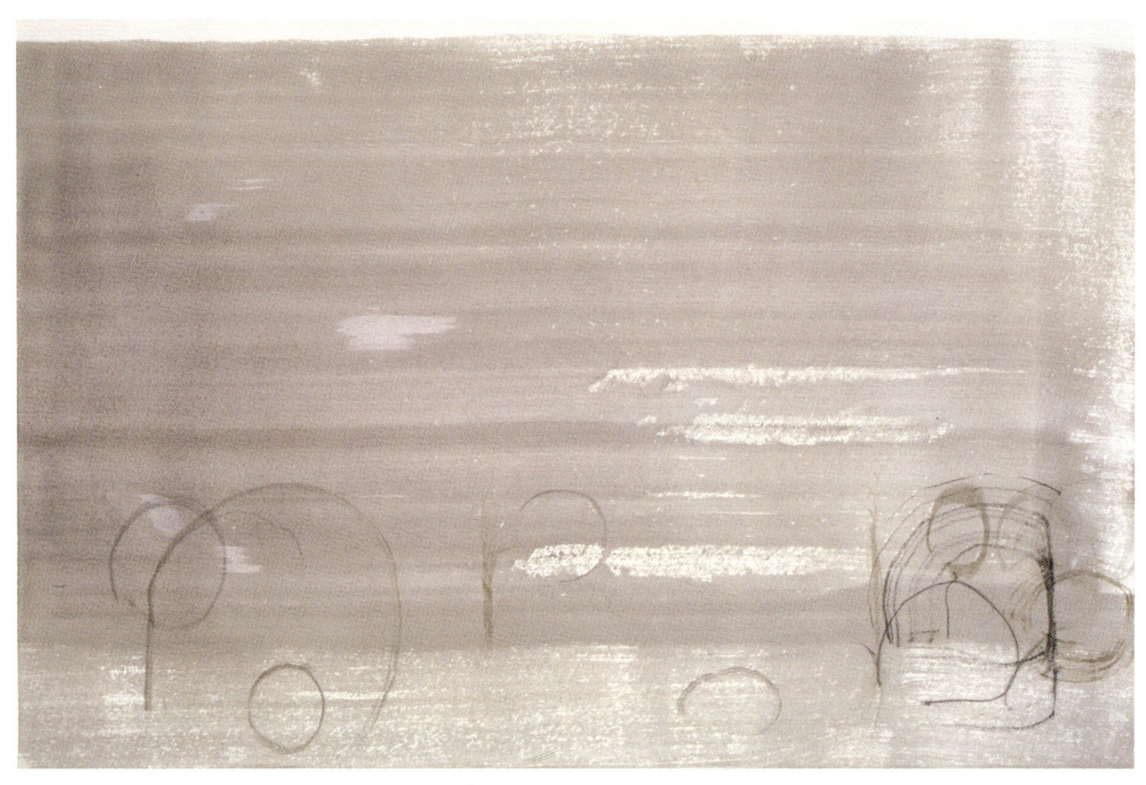

New River Watercolors, Series IV, No.2, 1988. *Watercolor on paper. 26-3/4 x 33-3/4" (66 x 86 cm).*

River Rocks and Smoke 4/10/90, No. 8. *Smoke and watercolor on paper. 72 x 48" (183 x 122 cm).*

each drawing was of a single stone (a single circle) in a thin wash. Then he made one painting that took a whole day and required 195 separate painting operations. Kass writes that he told Cage he was "disappointed" that the workshop's progress "would obviously be slowed by such a detailed painting."[40]

I asked Margarete Roeder, Cage's art dealer and a person he talked with about his art, if she thought Kass had intruded his own desires into the project. "I might be inclined to think so," she answered, "but I know John and even when he appears suggestible he does what he wants." She spoke touchingly in the present tense though it should have been the past. "And, don't forget," she added, "that there was a big physical involvement here." It's true. Cage did some of the watercolors when he was 76, some when he was 78. They range in size from 18 x 36" (46 x 92 cm) to almost eight feet tall and thirty feet long (2-1/2 x 9 meters). I can almost hear him saying, as he often did with laughter, "Isn't it amazing?"

In 1990, in his second workshop at Mountain Lake (seven days), Cage produced 61 works titled *River Rocks and Smoke.* He used smoke instead of washes to give tone to the watercolors. "This work has a great sense of quietness, and the stone tracings are especially energetic and free," comments Roeder, who placed many of the watercolors with clients of her gallery.

After the second workshop, Cage told Retallack, he had no more reservations. "Now my experience has changed," he said, "so that I feel all right with watercolor and brushes. In fact, I wouldn't be averse to working with them again. The reason is that in the workshop it's quite impossible to see what you're doing. It's flat rather than vertical, and you're not far away enough to see if it's very big. But I was at an exhibition in Wisconsin where I was able to see that [large] watercolor from a distance. And I liked it, just as others did. I enjoyed it."[41]

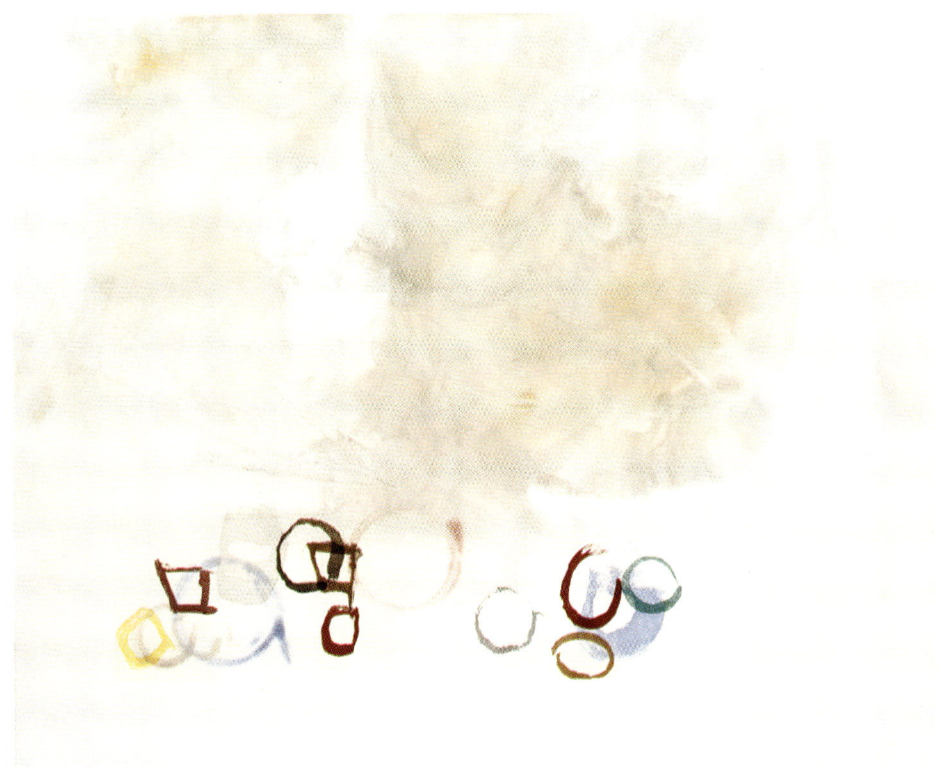

10 Stones, *1989. Aquatint on smoked paper printed by Marcia Bartholme at Crown Point Press in an edition of 20. 18 x 23" (46 x 59 cm).*

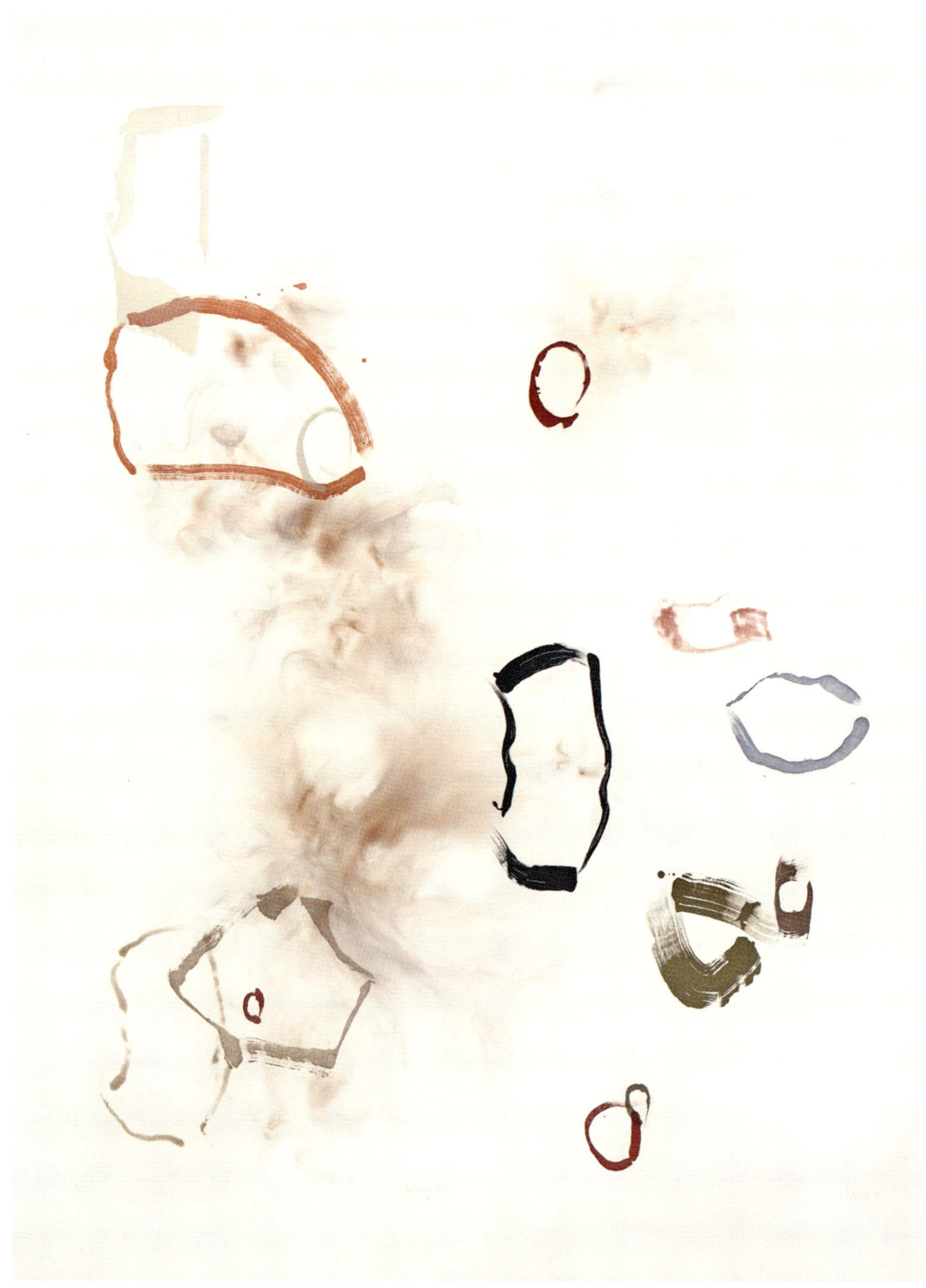

The Missing Stone, 1989. *Aquatint on smoked paper printed by Marcia Bartholme at Crown Point Press in an edition of 25. 54 x 41" (137 x 104 cm).*

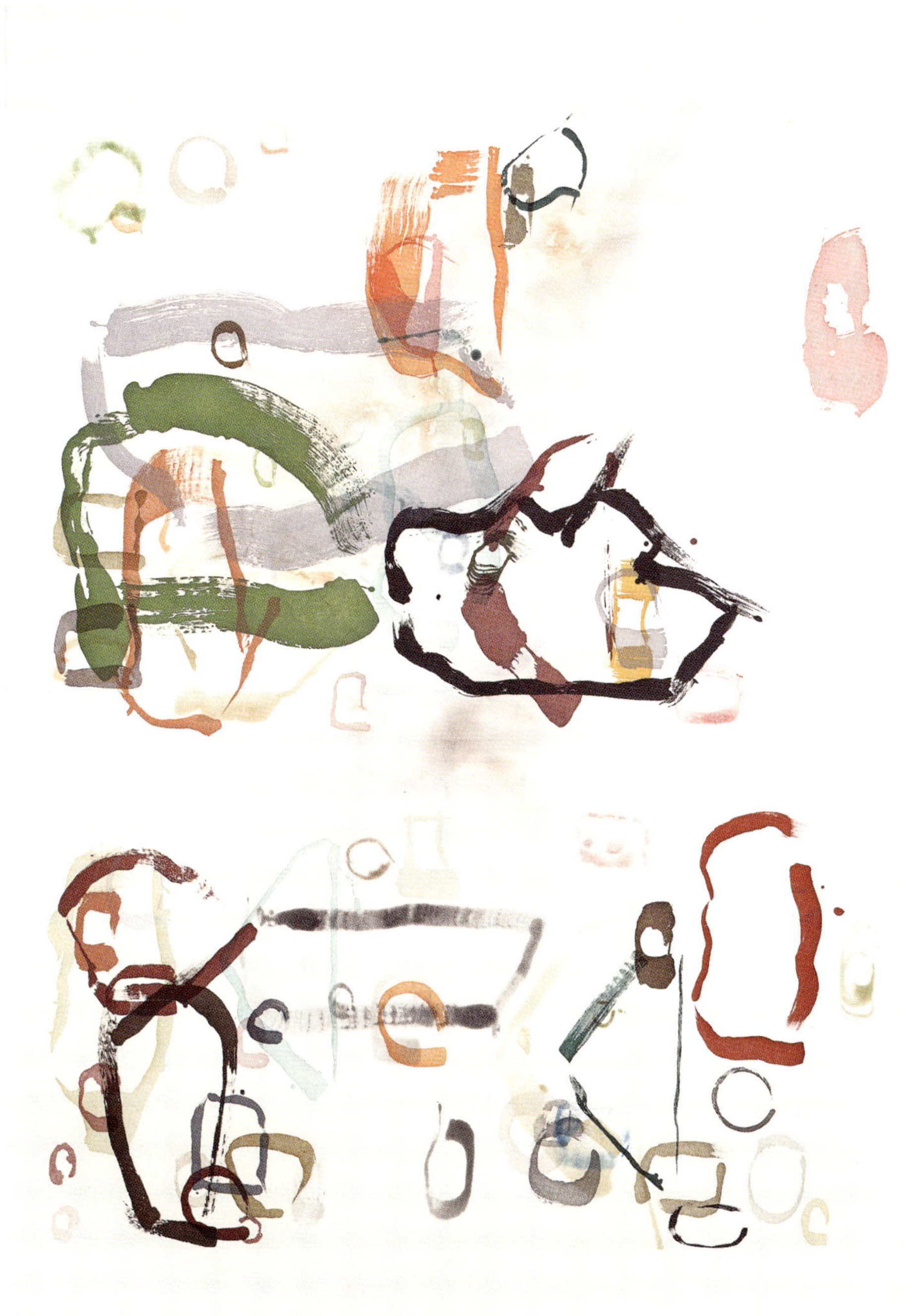

75 **Stones**, 1989. *Aquatint on smoked paper printed by Marcia Bartholme at Crown Point Press in an edition of 25. 54 x 41" (137 x 104 cm).*

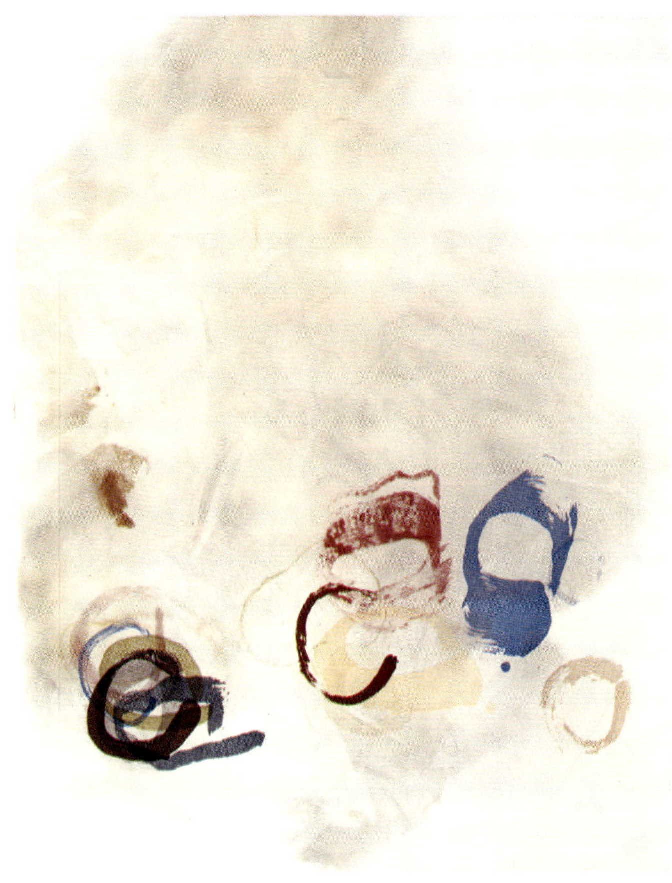

10 **Stones 2**, 1989. *Aquatint printed on smoked paper by Marcia Bartholme at Crown Point Press in an edition of 20. 23 x 18" (58 x 46 cm).*

IV. THE WAY WE SEE WEATHER

> If you disconnect [art] from both feeling and sense, from having something to say, and believing or feeling the truth of what you say, then it's quite different. …Benefits only arise when you don't have a thing in your head, or in your heart. Which doesn't mean that my head and my heart aren't any longer functioning. They function, you might put it, at different times, in different ways.
>
> —John Cage in conversation with Joan Retallack, July 16, 1992.[42]

The Final Prints: Crown Point Press, San Francisco, 1989, 1991, 1992. Because of his experience at Mountain Lake, Cage used brushes at Crown Point for the first time in 1989. In his work with us that year he made eight *Stones* prints, two of them quite large as etchings go. Like the watercolors that immediately preceded and followed them, the *Stones* prints are concerned with *method*. Cage was learning about brushmarks, and working them into his ideas about *structure*. But these prints and watercolors were a prelude to work that leaves structure largely behind.

Smoke Weather Stone Weather, a group of thirty-seven prints made in 1991, is a turning point between the structured watercolors and *Stones* prints and the simple openness of Cage's last works. Like *Déreau* and *Ryoku*, *Smoke Weather Stone Weather* seemed just to happen, and anticipated a change. We used unusual handmade paper and the number of sheets available determined the number of prints; we made only one impression of each image.

Cage combined brush drawings with an etched line that emphasizes the irregular quality of the stones. Eleven to fifteen stone tracings occupy each print and the images, without fragmenting, move around the paper and up to the edges. The

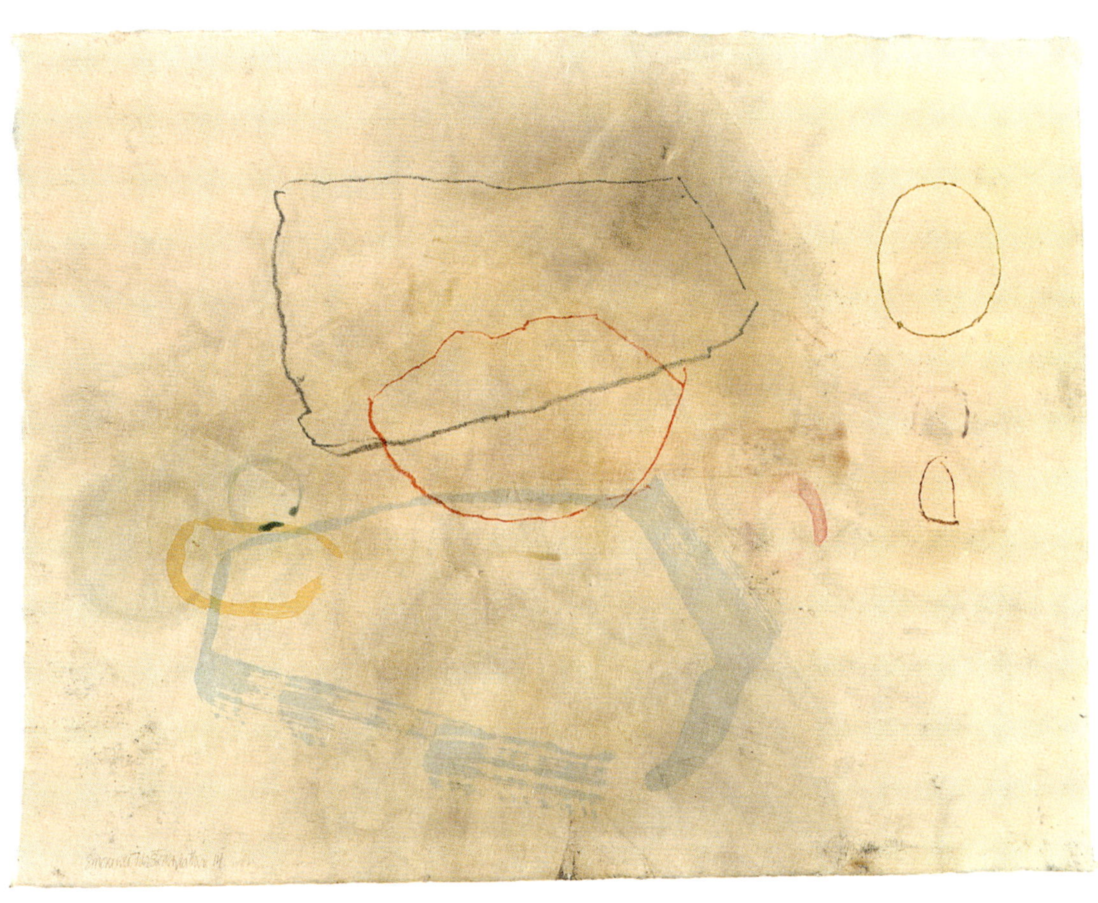

Smoke Weather Stone Weather 14, 1991. *One in a series of 37 unique aquatints with etching on smoked paper. Printed by Paul Mullowney at Crown Point Press. 15-1/2 x 20" (40 x 51 cm).*

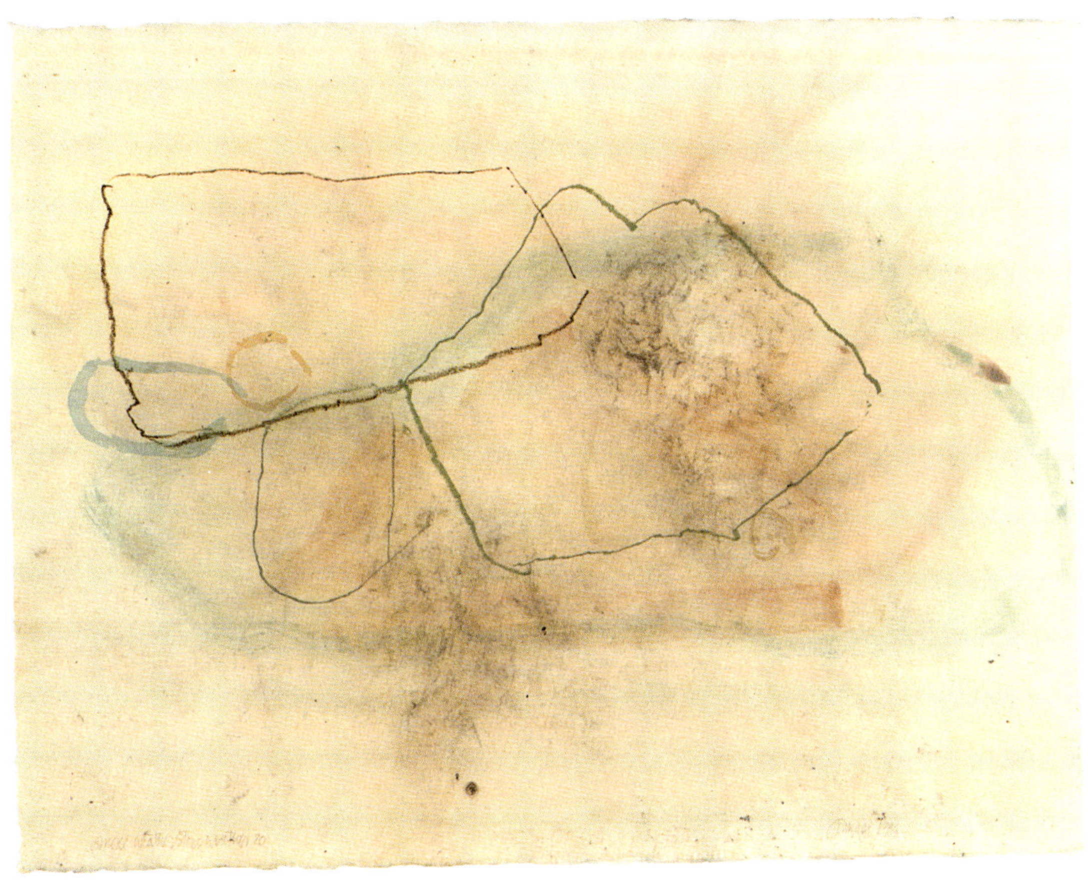

Smoke Weather Stone Weather 20, *unique*

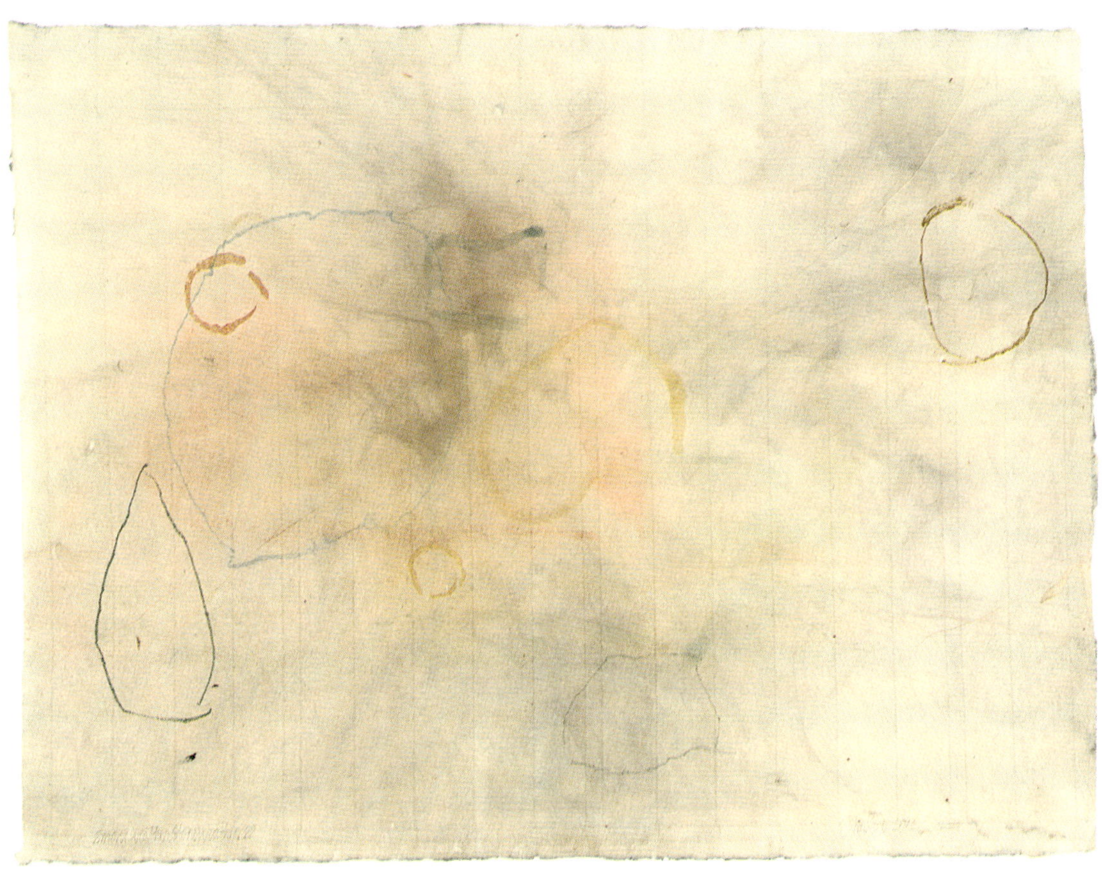

Smoke Weather Stone Weather 22, *unique*

colors are fragile and the paper smoked, so the figures both submerge into and emerge from the whole.

"I didn't want to have an image that would separate itself from the paper," Cage says on videotape I made in our studio in 1991. He is standing by the press speaking with a visitor as the printer cranks plate after plate through (each print had at least eleven runs). "I wanted to have an ambiguity between the smoke and the images. I was afraid at the beginning some of the marks were going to be too strong. But as we continue [smiling with delight and gesturing toward the press] even the strong marks loose anything that you could compare with impact."

Cage's title, *Smoke Weather Stone Weather,* shows his thinking at the time. The stone-drawings normally would provide

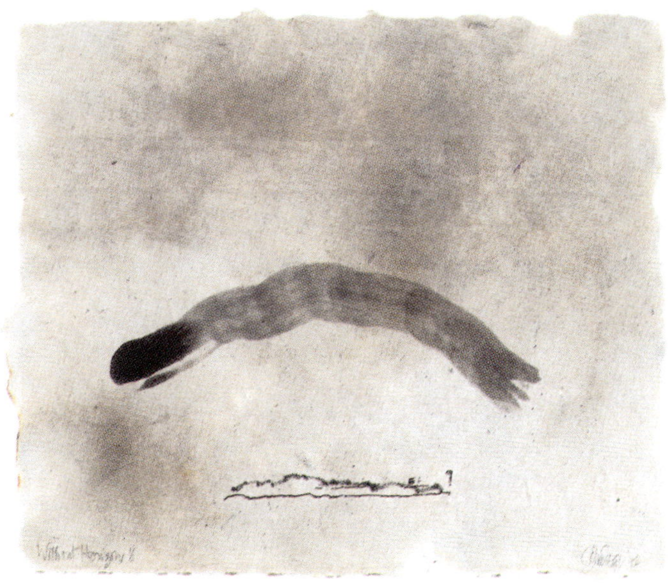

Without Horizon 8, 1992. *One in a series of 57 unique aquatints with etching and drypoint on smoked paper printed by Pamela Paulson at Crown Point Press. 7-1/2 x 8-1/2" (19 x 22 cm).*

structure, but here most of them slip away from structure and, like the smoke, become parts of the weather. Just a few drift into prominence in any single print. Cage told Retallack in 1992 that he thought of structure as something that could be divided into parts, whereas "weather remains the weather no matter what is going on…so that the structural elements that do appear don't change the way we *see* weather." He added that he was "having more and more the feeling of not being involved with structure."[43]

After fifteen years of art-making, Cage's attitudes had shifted. Here, again, are the ten words he listed in *Composition in Retrospect*: *method, structure, intention, discipline, notation, indeterminancy, interpenetration, imitation, devotion,* and *circumstances.* Over time, his art had become simpler as *method, structure, intention, notation,* and *imitation* waned in influence. *Discipline* had become less labored but not less present. *Interpenetration* had become stronger as images integrated with "weather." And *indeterminancy, circumstances,* and *devotion* had remained steady, always at the center of his work.

I read an interesting remark recently in a *New York Times* interview with a famous novelist. The novelist said, "If you're writing, you're not living, and if you're living, you're not writing."[44] She neatly defined the way many artists make art. They retreat into a separate world of their own creation, and then—if they are good enough—entice us into that world through their work. This is an example of art that Cage described as special, or "dressed up." His own approach was exactly the opposite. His work was part of living. It was more concentrated in its detail and more refined in its discipline than everyday life, but nonetheless it was integral to it, as the spirit is integral to the body.

Cage was not the only contemporary artist to integrate art and life—think of the artists who most influenced him, Marcel Duchamp and Mark Tobey. Following them are

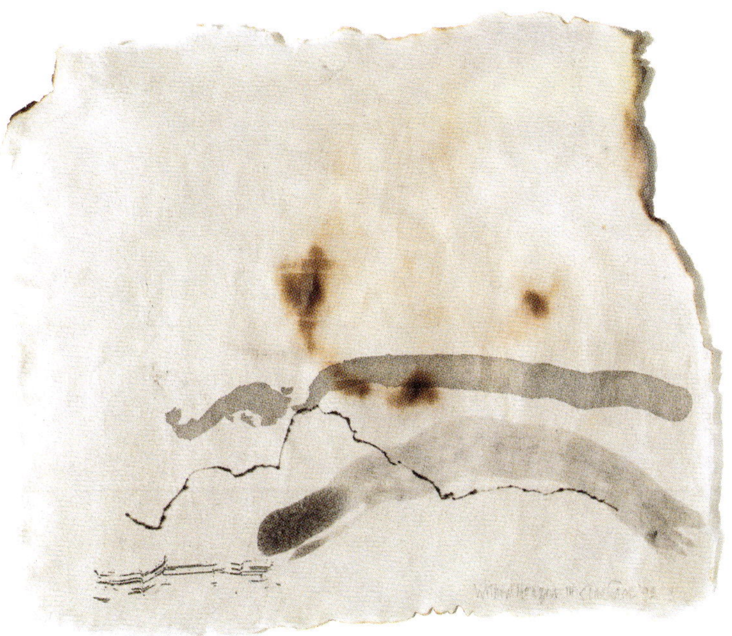

Without Horizon 14, *unique.*

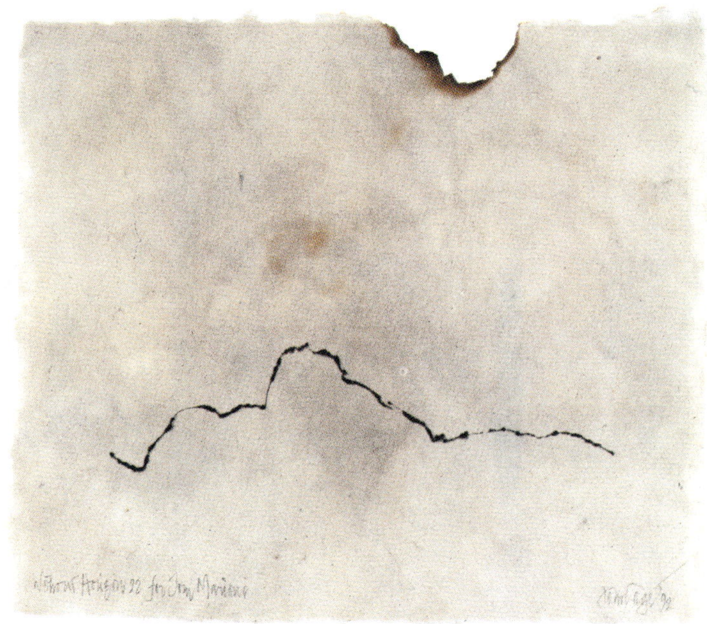

Without Horizon 22, *unique.*

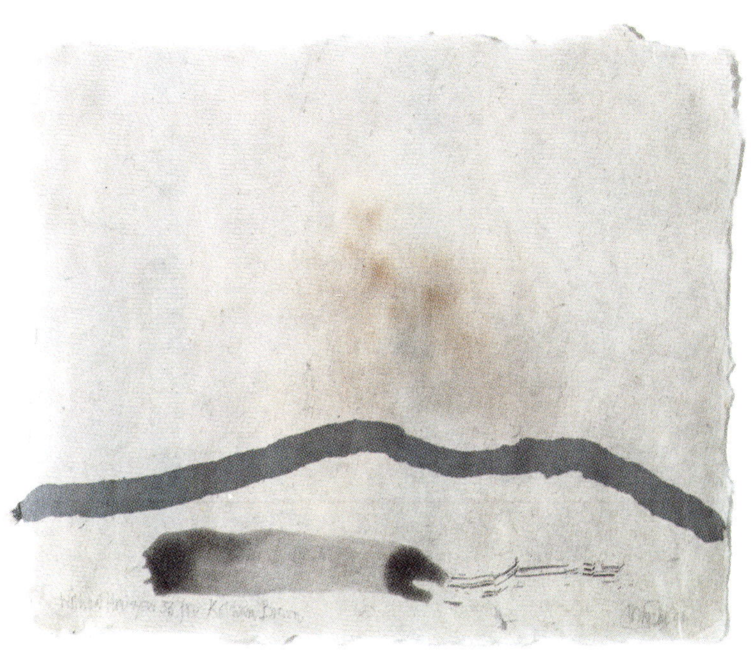

Without Horizon 33, *unique.*

others, some of whom are influenced by Cage. Their work does not manipulate the viewer. Nothing tells you how you are expected to react. Seduction by this type of art is gradual, and is likely to occur only after a person has taken some time with a first encounter. If it does occur, it can change the way you look at other things besides art by adding a spiritual, or out-of-the-ordinary, dimension that gives pleasure and quiets the mind's chatter.

Cage often said that the music and art he most enjoyed encourage paying attention as a way of being present in the world. He explained the idea to Joan Retallack like this: after leaving an exhibition of Mark Tobey's work, he "happened to look at the pavement, and—literally—the pavement was as beautiful as the Tobey. So the experience of looking at the Tobey was instructive about looking at the pavement. ...Art became identical with life."[45]

In Cage's work period with us in January 1992, he used his stones, but (relaxing his structure) he did not locate them by using a grid. On the press bed he centered each mark in the lower third of a defined space the size of the paper. Then, before printing, he moved the paper: up, down, left, or right according to chance operations. Instead of drawing around the stones, he drew along their edges. He made a series of 57 small prints on handmade gray smoked paper printed with black and gray inks. The series is called *Without Horizon*. Each print has one, three, four, or five marks that move independently to create an enormous landscape-like form in a very small space.

Cage did another series that January, also. He worked with plates that had been marked accidentally and with them he made a set of prints called *HV2*. He returned to using plates from our scrap pile, as he had done for the large set, *On the Surface* ten years earlier. The two sets are very different. *HV2* does not have the "musical" intricacy and internal movement of *On the Surface*. *HV2* is, in fact, not intricate, and it is very still. Its movement is something like breathing and drifts out beyond the paper's boundaries, then pulls inward again. Of all Cage's prints, I think this series does the most perfect job of sobering and quieting the mind, placing it, as he said to me on my first meeting with him, "in accord with what happens."

Each *HV2* print is filled completely with horizontal and vertical rectangles of varying sizes in transparent colors, all the colors essentially the same density. The plates were left uncleaned prior to etching, and the accumulated oils from fingers and hands that touched them before and after they were taken from the scrap pile left permanent marks. The colors glow evenly except for these lighter smudges and fingermarks. Other marks, darker ones, are the nicks and scratches and occasional lines that Cage expected would come, as he said, "from existence."

Cage had asked us that year, 1992, to plan the work so everything could be completed in the two weeks he was with us. That is why *HV2* is a small set, only fifteen prints. In constructing an image, Cage first pulled plates from the scrap pile, working quickly and not studying them, but not using his *I Ching* materials. He laid the plates out horizontally and vertically on paper the size of the sheet we would use for printing. If he picked up a plate that was unwieldy or obviously already marked, he put it on the plate cutter, jumped on the treadle to lower the blade, and cut off the part he could not use.

He subjected each plate to chance operations to obtain its color mixture, and recorded the mixtures in a score the printers could follow. Then he drew a map showing the positions of the plates. After the plates had been etched and inked by the printers, he used the map as a guide for reassembling the image on the press bed. We made three prints of each of the fifteen images. One set, at Cage's request, has been kept together.

While work on *HV2* was going on, we were also working on *Without Horizon,* the small gray prints that resemble landscapes. We made as many of these as possible in the time we had, and printed only one of each.

It turned out that *Without Horizon* and *HV2* were the last etchings John Cage would make. He died later that year, on August 12, twenty-four days before his 80th birthday.

NOTES

[1] Retallack, Joan, ed. *Musicage: Cage Muses on Words, Art, Music.* Wesleyan University Press, Hanover, NH, 1996. p. 106.
[2] To augment my memory of this, I found it in print in "Composition in Retrospect," *John Cage Etchings 1978-1982,* Crown Point Press, San Francisco, 1982. p. 43.
[3] *One[11],* 1992.
[4] Sylvester, David, "Points in Space," *Dancers on a Plane: Cage, Cunningham, Johns,* Anthony d'Offay Gallery, London, 1989. p. 50.
[5] Retallack, p. 110.
[6] Retallack, p. 127.
[7] White, Robin, "Interview with John Cage," *View,* Vol. 1, No. 1, Apr. 1978, Crown Point Press, Oakland, CA. p. 15.
[8] Kotz, Mary Lynn, *Rauschenberg/Art and Life,* Harry N. Abrams, New York, 1990. p. 89.
[9] Retallack, p. 106.
[10] Retallack, p. 121.
[11] Sylvester, p. 47.
[12] Retallack, p. 139.
[13] From a videotape I made, 1979.
[14] Johnson, George, "Hardly Dead, Physics Lives Out a Permanent Revolution," *The New York Times,* June 20, 2000, New York. p. D6.
[15] Cage, John, "Composition in Retrospect," *John Cage Etchings 1978-1982,* Crown Point Press, San Francisco, 1982. pp. 39-57. Cage expanded this text and made it the basis for *The Norton Lectures* at Harvard University in 1988 and 1989.
[16] White, p. 12.
[17] I got this quote from a label on a black painting of Rauschenberg's at the San Francisco Museum of Modern Art, 2000.
[18] Retallack, p. 93.
[19] Retallack, p. 127. The full context here is the quote about Mark Tobey cited as footnote 4.
[20] Retallack, p. 93.
[21] Cage, John, *IV,* Harvard University Press, Boston, 1990. pp. 66-73. This part of the text is not punctuated. I have added punctuation for readability.
[22] Retallack, p. 92.
[23] Retallack, p. 95.
[24] From a videotape I made, 1978.
[25] White, p. 5.
[26] White, p. 6.
[27] Retallack, p. 96.
[28] From a videotape I made, 1979.
[29] Cage, John, in Kostelanetz, Richard, ed. "An Autobiographical Statement (1989)," *John Cage Writer: Previously Uncollected Pieces,* Limelight Editions, NY, 1993, p. 245.
[30] Retallack, p. 96.
[31] Retallack, p. 209
[32] Cage, John, "How to Pass, Kick, Fall, and Run," *A Year from Monday,* Wesleyan University Press, Middletown, CT, first published 1963, third printing, 1975, p. 133.
[33] Cage, John, "Rhythm, Etc.," *A Year from Monday,* p. 123.
[34] Kostelanetz, p. 135.
[35] Retallack, p. 138.
[36] Retallack, p. 242.
[37] From a videotape I made in 1986.
[38] Kass, Ray, "The Mountain Lake Workshop," *John Cage/New River Watercolors,* Virginia Museum of Fine Arts, Richmond, VA, 1988. p. 2.
[39] Kass, p. 9.
[40] Kass p. 13.
[41] Retallack, p. 141.
[42] Retallack, pp. 216-217.
[43] Retallack, p. 197.
[44] Margaret Atwood in an interview with Mel Gussow, *New York Times,* October 10, 2000.
[45] Retallack, p. 101.

HV2
1992

Fifteen aquatints printed in three impressions each by Pamela Paulson at Crown Point Press. 12 x 14" (30 x 36 cm). The numbers in each print's title are not sequential. They refer to the number of plates in the print.

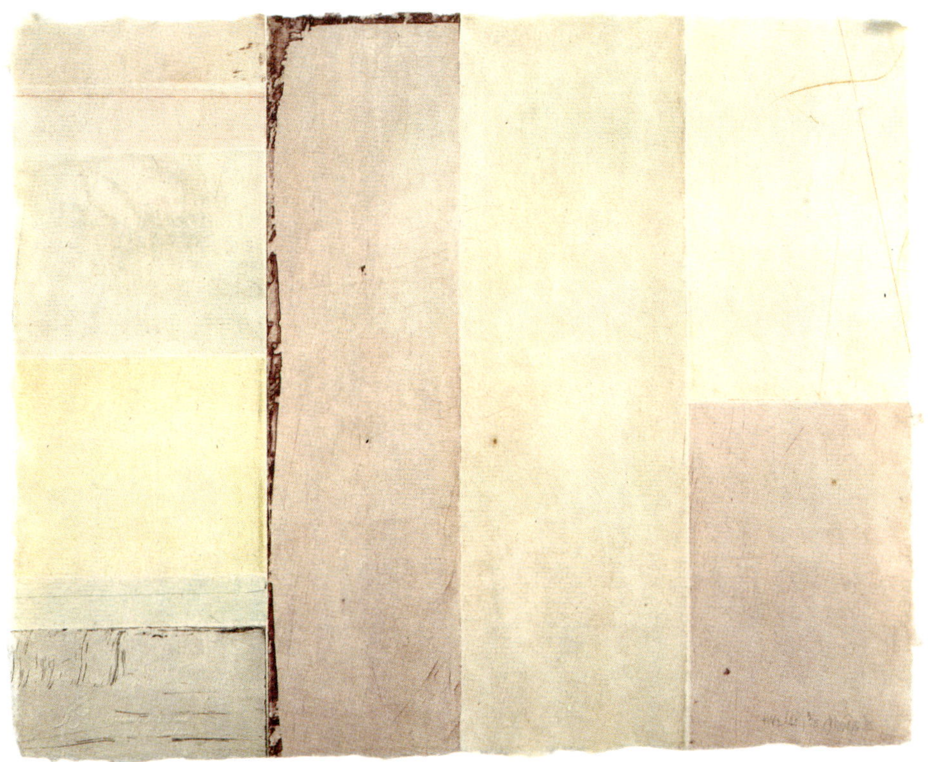

HV2 10

HV2 14

HV2 14B

HV2 14c

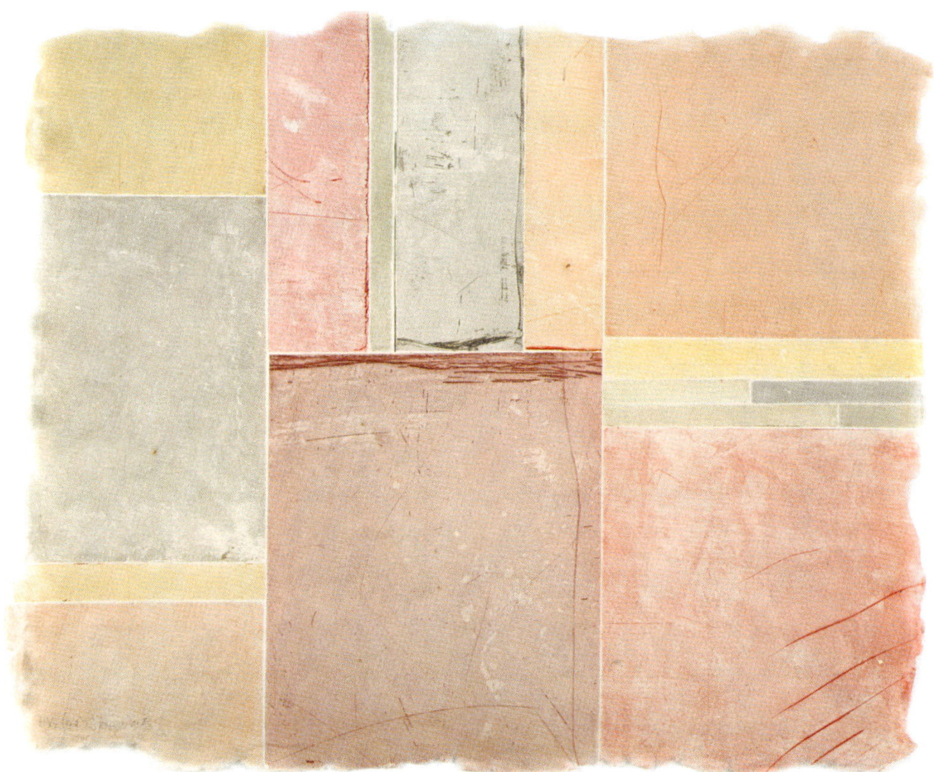

HV2 17A

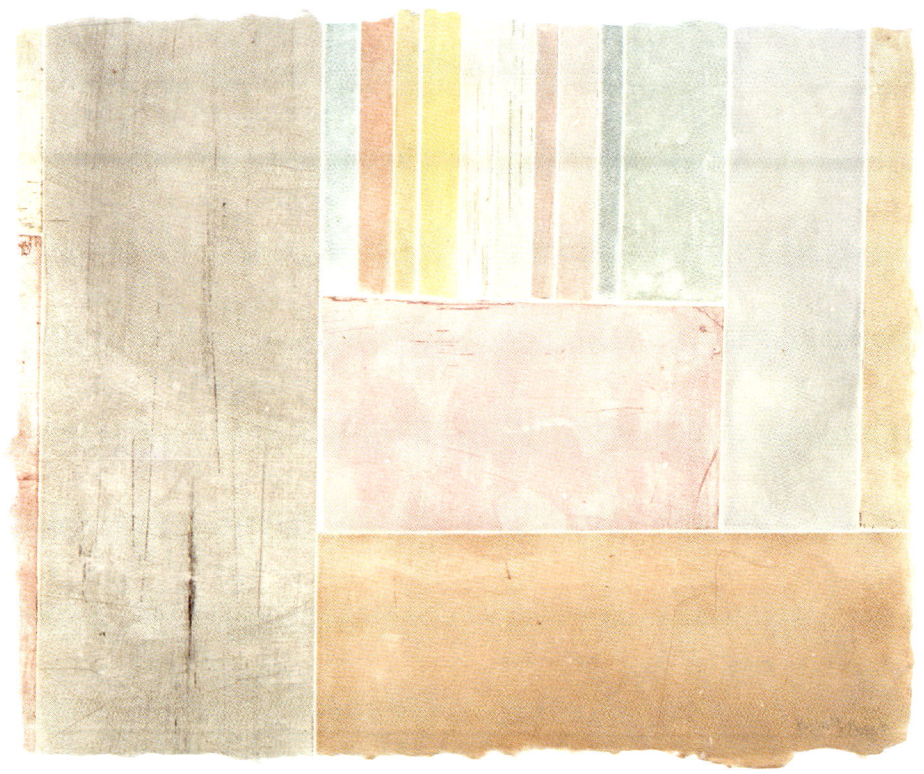

HV2 17B

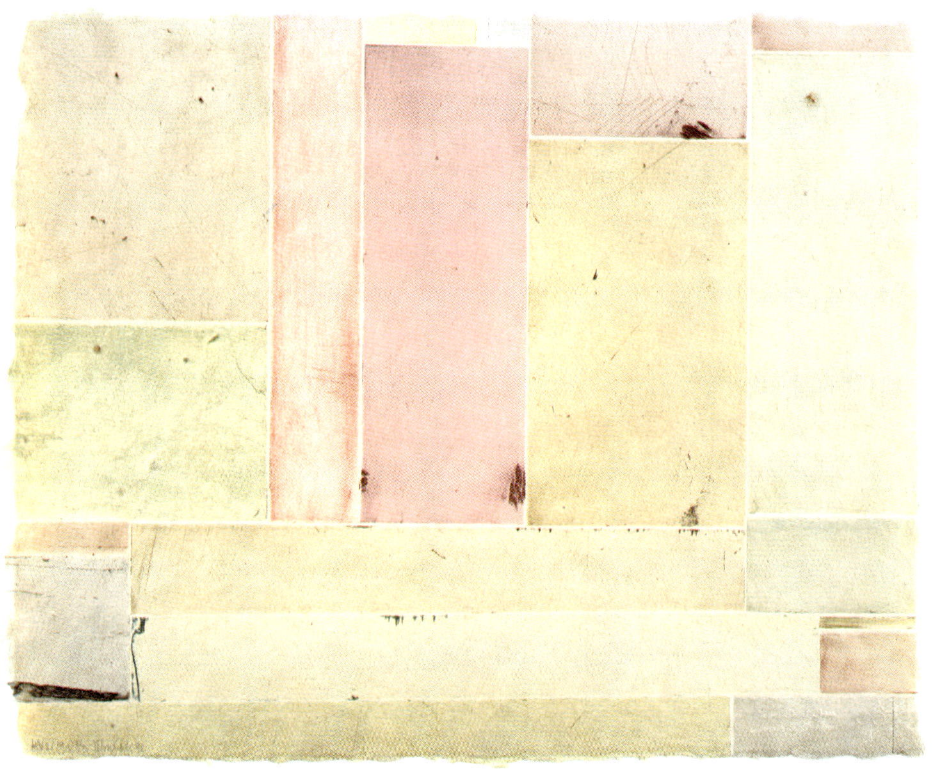

HV2 19A

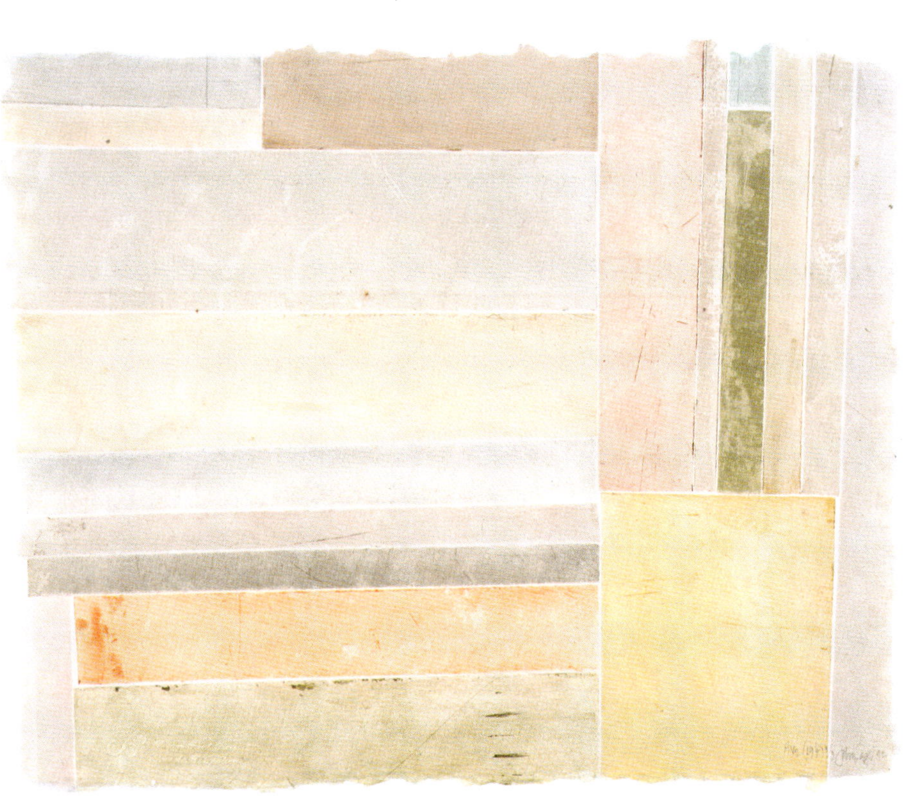

HV2 19B

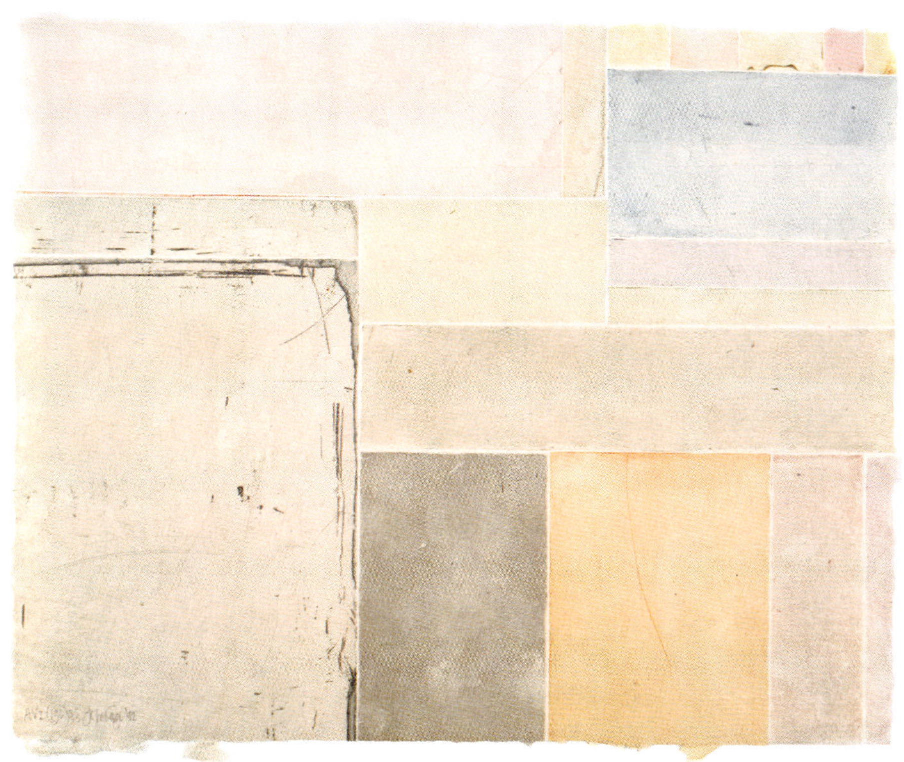

HV2 19C

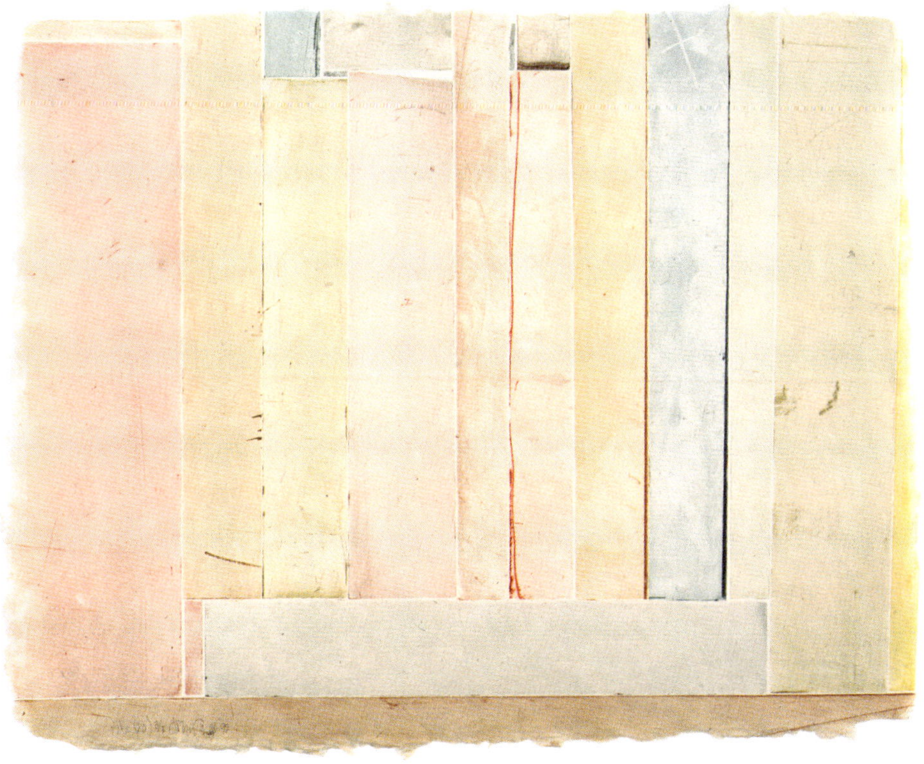

HV2 20

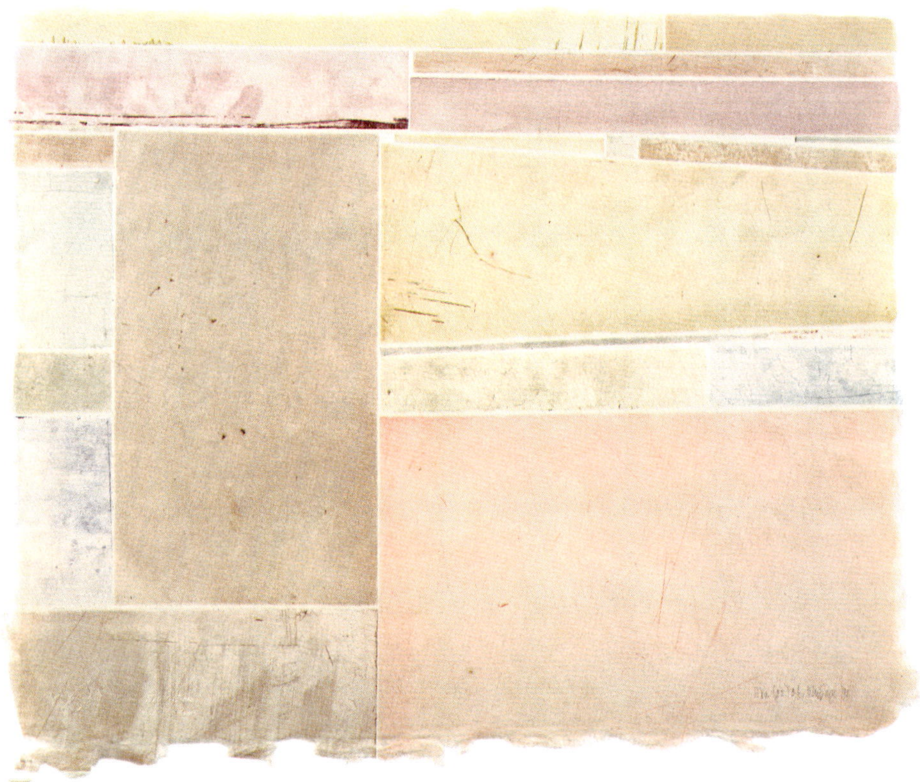

HV2 22

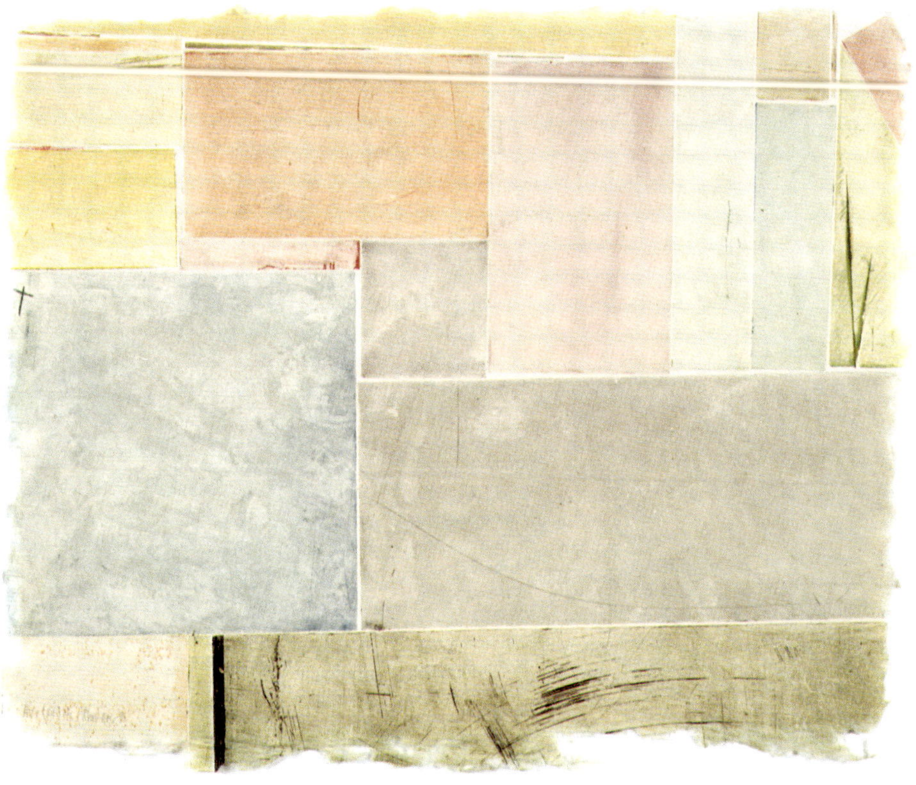

HV2 24

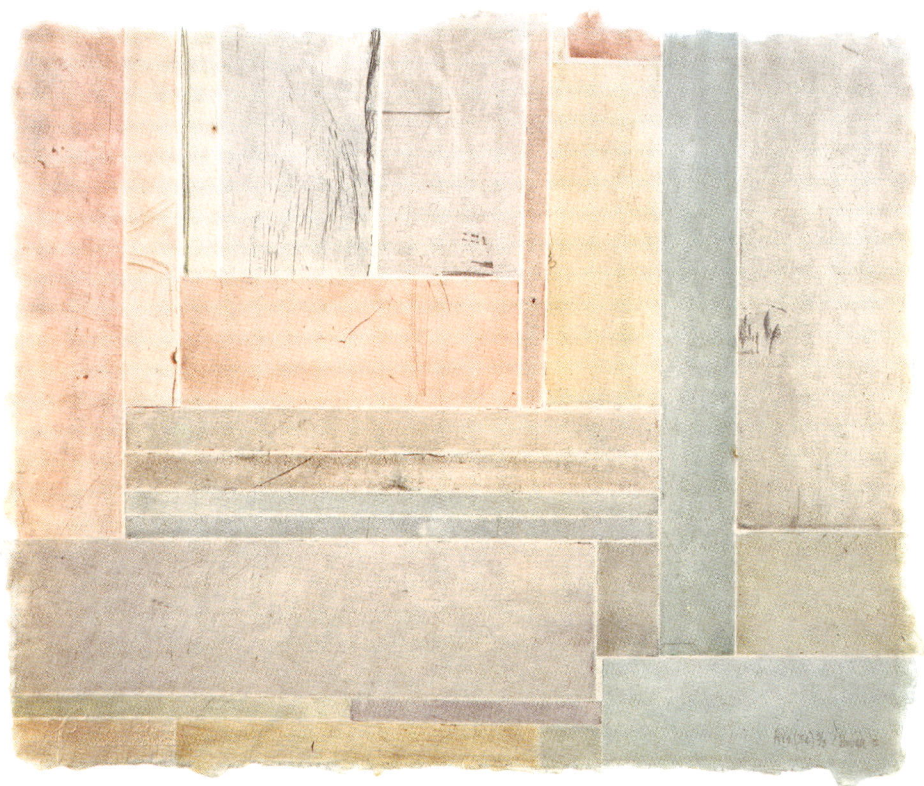

HV2 25A

HV2 25B

HV2 6

to sober and quiet the minD
so that It
iS
in aCcord
wIth
what haPpens
the worLd
around It
opeN
rathEr than

closeD
goIng in
by Sitting
Crosslegged
returnIng
to daily exPerience
with a smiLe
gIft
giviNg no why
aftEr emptiness

"You know this or that, or you don't know it. All important or not important. It brings to mind the marvelous story in the world of Zen Buddhism where the man is standing on the hill in the distance and a group of people come along and see him standing there and begin to wonder why he's standing there. When they finally reach him, they say we've been having this discussion about why you're standing here. Which one of us is right? He says, I have no reason, I'm just standing here."

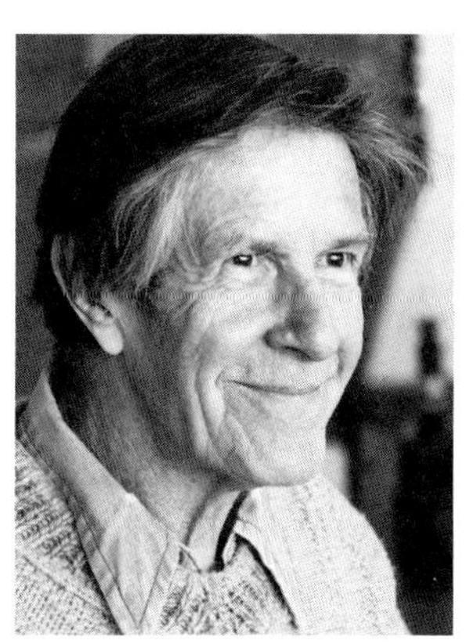